Contents

Colour Plates

THE
STORY OF
WEDGWOOD

Compiled by Alison Kelly in association with
Josiah Wedgwood & Sons Ltd

A STUDIO BOOK

THE VIKING PRESS • NEW YORK

Monochrome Plates

22. Early period kitchen ware in Queen's Ware, c. 1790.

23. Drawing of a Queen's Ware jelly mould, illustrated in 1802 shape book.

24. Agricultural implements are used as decoration on items in Queen's Ware tableware, c. 1805.

25. Queen's Ware plate decorated with 'Water Lily' pattern.

26. Plate and jug in Queen's Ware, with underglaze decoration.

27. Queen's Ware gravy dish and cover. From a service ordered by Lord William Russell in 1815.

28. These plates illustrate three patterns used to decorate Queen's Ware services in the period 1820–30.

29. Potpourri container, bowl and jug in Queen's Ware, with drab (olive green) glaze.

30. Stone china dish, decorated with underglaze 'Blue Claude' pattern, c. 1830.

31. Dish from an armorial Queen's Ware service commissioned by the Duke of Clarence (later William IV) in 1821.

32. Ruined classical column in cane ware, decorated with reliefs of sphinxes, sacrifices, etc. around plinth, c. 1800.

33. Cane ware cabaret service with hand-enamelled border pattern, c. 1790.

34. Inkwell in the form of a canopic jar. In cane ware, with applied brown reliefs in imitation of Egyptian hieroglyphics, c. 1800.

35. Game pie dish in cane ware, c. 1810. Unglazed, in a soft buff—and made to resemble a pastry case.

36. Cane ware oil and vinegar set, shaped to look like a boat with swan's head terminals.

37. Eighteenth-century portrait medallions in Jasper.

38. Jasper plaque, illustrating 'The Apotheosis of Homer', designed and modelled by John Flaxman RA.

39. The 'Dancing Hours'—a Jasper frieze arranged in two panels, designed by John Flaxman and first mentioned by Wedgwood in April 1778.

40. A rook from Flaxman's Jasper chess set.

41. John Flaxman's original drawings for his chessmen, designed in 1784.

42. The 'Homer' vase, in white on dark blue Jasper.

43. Diced Jasper vase and jug. Both coloured in blue, green and white, c. 1785.

44. The Sydney Cove Medallion, in Jasper. Issued in 1789 to mark the foundation of Sydney.

45. Two buttons, in white Jasper with blue dip (surface only colouring), c. 1790.

46. Chatelaine, or fob chain, with blue and white Jasper cameos mounted in cut steel, c. 1790.

47. Two black and white Jasper vases from a garniture de cheminée, c. 1790.

48. Blue Jasper vase on pedestal, c. 1850. Copy of famous Borghese Vase, with white relief decoration showing 'The Triumph of Bacchus'.

49. A selection of 'Moonlight' and 'Steel' lustre ware.

50. First period bone china. Coffee can and saucer decorated in Wedgwood pattern No. 637.

51. Fine bone china tea service items, including oval parapet teapot.

52. 'Chinese Tigers', the name of a vivid green pattern, edged with gold.

53. Simple Yet Perfect (SYP) teapot, c. 1907. An original teapot design introduced by Wedgwood in 1895.

54. Queen's Ware jug and dolphin candlestick decorated with 'Majolica' glaze, c. 1865.

55. Five items of Queen's Ware decorated by Emile Lessore, the eminent artist who worked for Wedgwood in England, 1858–63.

56. 'Ambition' is the title of this hand-enamelled design, on a Queen's Ware vase, by the painter, Walter Crane.

57. Bowl and vases in 'Fairyland Lustre' and 'Dragon Ware'.

58. 'Fairyland Lustre' plaque entitled 'Bubbles'. Designed by Daisy Makeig-Jones c. 1920.

59. Queen's Ware animals, modelled by the sculptor John Skeaping.

60. The Boat Race cup, decorated with multi-coloured printed design on Queen's Ware.

61. 'The Mexicans'—a pair of candlesticks designed by Professor Angelo Biancini. Produced in terracotta and Black Basalt, in 1962.

62. Two designs from 'Variations on a Geometric Theme', a set of six bone china plates designed by the sculptor and graphic artist, Eduardo Paolozzi.

The First Wedgwood Potters

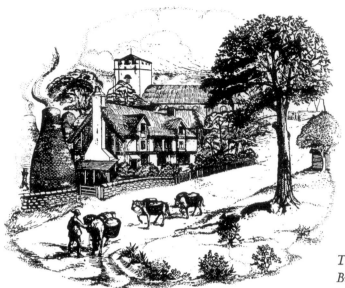

The Churchyard House and Works, Burslem

JOSIAH WEDGWOOD was born in Burslem, at that time the only township in 'the Potteries' district of North Staffordshire. He was the thirteenth, and youngest, child of Thomas and Mary Wedgwood, of the Churchyard Pottery. The exact date of his birth is not known but he was christened on July 12th, 1730, at Burslem parish church, where the entry of his name can still be seen in the register. In those days of high infant mortality little time elapsed between a birth and a baptism.

He came from a family of yeoman copyholders, who can be traced back to the thirteenth century, and who lived a few miles north of Burslem, where a farm named Wedgwood exists to this day. Josiah's great-great-grandfather, Gilbert, came to live in Burslem after his marriage to Margaret Burslem, the heiress of the Squire of that time, and through her he inherited an estate of about two hundred acres.

In the marriage settlement of his son Moses, in 1649, a document which is in the Wedgwood Museum archives at Barlaston, Gilbert describes himself as a master potter. This, however, is all that is known of him as a potter, and it was his second son Thomas, Josiah's great-grandfather, who can claim to have established the family in the pottery industry. Thomas, a 'yeoman' and 'gentleman', inherited a potworks in 1656, which he managed so well that he built a new factory, the Churchyard Works, next to Burslem church. This factory was inherited in turn by Josiah's grandfather and father, both called Thomas. When Josiah's father died, the Churchyard Works passed to Josiah's elder brother, also Thomas, and in 1780 Josiah bought it from his nephew, yet another Thomas.

Altogether, four of Gilbert Wedgwood's descendants became potters, and among them contributed to the advancement of the craft. Josiah's cousin, Dr. Thomas Wedgwood (1695–1737) achieved a considerable reputation for his salt-glazed ware. Josiah's uncles, John and Thomas, were the first to employ travellers and to trade directly with London and Liverpool, instead of selling their ware to hawkers. They also invented pyrometrical beads for measuring the temperatures of their ovens.

Josiah was only nine years old at the time of the death of his father who had not been a successful potter. In his will he left £20 to each of his seven surviving children, but payment was not made until the 1770's.

Josiah's mother, Mary, was the daughter of a Mr. Stringer, Unitarian minister of Newcastle-under-Lyme. She was thus better educated than most of the daughters of farmers and potters of those days.

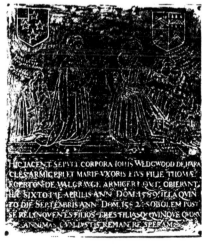

Wedgwood brass in Horton church

'Here lie buried the bodies of John Wedgwood of Haracles Esquire and of Mary his wife, daughter of Thomas Egerton of Walgrange Esquire He died this sixth day of April in the year of our Lord 1589 She on the fifth of September in the year of our Lord 1582 leaving issue, three sons and five daughters Let us hope that their souls will rest with the Righteous'

The Days of Salt-Glaze and Pack-Horses

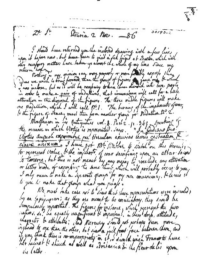

*One of Josiah Wedgwood's letters
(dated November 2nd 1786).
He was 'master of a capital hand'*

JOSIAH's education began when he was six years old. He attended a school in Newcastle-under-Lyme kept by Thomas Blunt, who, according to his biographer, Miss Meteyard, made him 'a fair arithmetician and master of a capital hand'. The quality of this hand, legible and graceful, can be seen in the letter reproduced above. It is worth recording that he walked, to school and back, seven miles a day.

When his father died in 1739 he left school to start work under his eldest brother, Thomas, who had succeeded as 'master' at the Churchyard Works. Five years later he became his brother's apprentice, to learn 'the Art, Mistery, Occupation or Imployment of Throwing and Handleing'.

Pottery manufacture was still a peasant craft. Thirty years earlier, there had been forty-two 'pot banks' in Burslem, seven in Hanley and two in Stoke. Each employed, on the average, less than a dozen workmen, and wages did not exceed six shillings a week. The profits of these potteries ranged from about £90 to nearly £300 a year, and it is estimated that the average was not more than £150. The only products were butter-pots, jugs and mugs in cloudy, mottled, black and red 'bodies' made from the local clays, and drab-coloured salt-glazed stonewares. Of the bewildering variety of table-wares which was to develop later in the century, and which is still the backbone of the pottery industry, there was then hardly a sign.

However, in the second quarter of the eighteenth century much technical progress had been made and sales had increased. Twenty years before Josiah Wedgwood's apprenticeship began, Astbury had introduced flint, and blue and white clays from Dorset and Devon, to obtain a whiter and finer 'body' than could be made from Staffordshire clay. By 1750 Enoch Booth had introduced a liquid lead glaze which gave a much smoother surface than could be achieved with salt-glaze.

In 1750 methods of production were still primitive and the district was isolated. Burslem, the only town, had five shops, and letters were delivered by an old woman every Sunday from Newcastle-under-Lyme. There was no turn-pike road. The few lanes which existed were impassable for carts; indeed, every journey was an adventure.

Buff and white clays from Dorset and Devon, flint and other materials were shipped to Chester or Liverpool and carried thence to North Staffordshire partly by pack-horse and partly by river.

Popular amusements were brutal, such as bull or bear-baiting and cock or dog-fighting. The manners and habits of the people were scathingly censured by John Wesley when he first visited the Potteries in about 1760. Even those who had left their cruder pastimes to hear him preach did not escape his criticism, although he seems to have been singularly patient. 'Deep attention sat on every face, though, as yet, accompanied by deep ignorance,' he writes of his congregation. 'The next day I preached at eight to near double the number, some quite innocent of thought; five or six were laughing or talking till I had near done, and one of them threw a clod of earth which struck me on the side of the head, but it neither disturbed me nor the congregation.' But Wesley noted one exception. 'I met a young man', he wrote, 'by the name of J. Wedgwood, who had planted a flower garden adjacent to his pottery. He also had his men wash their hands and faces and change their clothes after working in the clay. He is small and lame, but his soul is near to God.'

Such were conditions when Josiah began to earn his living.

When approaching his twelfth year, Josiah got smallpox, with the rest of his family. In his case, it was a very virulent attack, which left him with an infection in the right knee. This improved, and at the age of fourteen, he was apprenticed as a thrower. However, between the ages of fifteen and sixteen, the trouble in his knee returned, and he was obliged to abandon throwing, and stay away from the pottery for some time. The letters and pamphlets he wrote in later life show, in their clarity of expression, and evidence of wide reading, that he was able to turn to good account this and many other periods of enforced retirement from active work.

At the end of his apprenticeship, in 1749, his brother Thomas refused to accept him as a partner. No documents now exist to explain Thomas's action, and it may be assumed that the reason for it lay in the different characters of the two brothers. Thomas had inherited a modest family business; he may well have been frightened of the driving imagination and spirit of experiment which he saw developing in his younger brother.

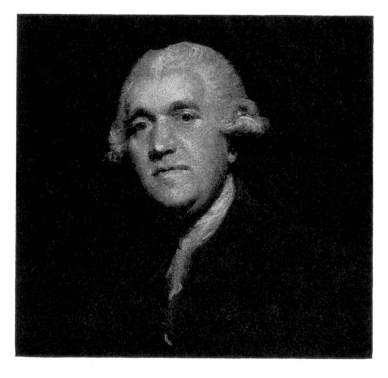

Josiah Wedgwood, FRS 1730–1795 from a portrait by Sir Joshua Reynolds PRA, 1782

The Partnership with Whieldon

'I SAW THE FIELD WAS SPACIOUS. . . .'

SINCE he could not work with his brother, Josiah had to find a partner outside his own family. In or about 1752, he went into partnership with John Harrison, a local tradesman and the son of a banker, who had acquired an interest in the pottery works of Thomas Alders at Cliffe Bank; but the agreement did not last long. Again, there may have been a lack of sympathy between the two men. An early account says that Harrison wished to restrict manufacture to marbled ware, salt-glaze ware and other traditional Staffordshire products which sold well at the time. Such a programme could hardly be acceptable to Josiah, but fortunately for him a better alternative was soon available.

In 1754 he entered into a partnership with Thomas Whieldon of Fenton, a potter of distinction and taste who had built up a good business. Whieldon was a liberal-minded man and, like his partner, had the same love of experiment, the same integrity, genial temperament and benevolence. It is evident from the clauses of the agreement and later correspondence that Wedgwood was free to pursue his researches without obligation to reveal to his partner how his results were achieved. Recent excavations at Fenton Vivian, near Fenton Low, have revealed many examples, in a wide variety of styles, of these early Whieldon–Wedgwood wares.

Towards the end of the partnership which terminated in 1759 he began to keep a record of his trials in his 'Experiment Book', from which the following is a quotation:

'This suite of Experiments was begun at Fenton Hall, in the parish of Stoke-on-Trent, about the beginning of the year 1759, in my partnership with Mr. Whieldon, for the improvement of our manufacture of earthenware, which at the time stood in great need of it, the demand for our goods decreasing daily, and the trade universally complained of as being bad and in a declining condition.

'White Stone Ware was the principal article of our manufacture. But this had been made a long time, and the prices were now reduced so low, that the potters could not afford to bestow much expense upon it or to make it so good in any respect as the ware would otherwise admit of. And with regard to Elegance of form, that was an object very little attended to.

'The next article in consequence to Stone Ware was an imitation of Tortoiseshell. But as no improvement had been made in this branch for several years, the country was grown weary of it; and though the price had been lowered from time to time in order to increase the sale, the expedient did not answer, and something new was wanted to give a little spirit to the business.

'I had already made an imitation of Agate, which was esteemed beautiful and a considerable improvement, but people were surfeited with wares of these variegated colours.

'These considerations induced me to try for some more solid improvements, as well in the Body as the Glazes, the Colours, and the Forms, of the articles of our manufacture.

'I saw the field was spacious, and the soil so good, as to promise an ample recompense to any one who should labour diligently in its cultivation.'

It should perhaps be explained that Josiah and his contemporaries made a distinction between agate ware on the one hand and tortoiseshell and marbled ware on the other. Tortoiseshell and marbled wares were made on a cream coloured clay base. This was dusted over with various oxides which, in the firing, ran into the glaze to produce streaky and mottled surfaces. Whieldon's name has been particularly associated with this type of ware. Agate ware, on the other hand, is made of different coloured clays kneaded, or to use the pottery term 'wedged', together, so that the marbled effect goes right through the piece.

Wedgwood in Business Alone

THE DEVELOPMENT OF
CREAM-COLOURED EARTHENWARE

IN 1759 Wedgwood started on his own account at the Ivy House Works in Burslem, which he rented for £10 a year from his prosperous relatives John and Thomas Wedgwood of the 'Big House', whose niece, Sarah, he was destined to marry. In the same year he engaged his cousin, Thomas, as manager. Josiah's first distinctive achievement as an independent potter was his invention of a green glaze. Its formula was No. 7 in Josiah's first experiment book, and against the entry he later wrote in the following comment:

'This No. is the result of many Expts. which I made in order to introduce a new species of coloured ware, to be fired along with the tortoiseshell and Agate wares, in our common gloss ovens, to be of an even self colour, and laid upon the ware in the form of a coloured glaze. This No. has been used for several years very successfully, in a great variety of articles both for home and foreign consumption.'

The invention of green glaze came at a particularly fortunate moment, since imitations of fruit and vegetables made in porcelain were greatly admired in the rococo taste of the mid-eighteenth century. With a good green glaze, it was possible to make pieces in earthenware in the same style. Cauliflowers and pineapples were imitated for teapots, and a whole series of plates, dishes and compotiers were designed in leaf shapes to show the green glaze off to the best advantage. Many of these are still made today.

In 1762 Josiah moved to the Brick House 'pot bank', also in Burslem, for which he paid a rent of £21 a year. Here he continued to manufacture 'useful' as distinct from 'ornamental' ware until 1773. This factory became known as the Bell Works, because the workmen were summoned by ringing a bell instead of by blowing a horn as was the custom in the district.

It was in the manufacture of 'useful' wares that Wedgwood first made his name. For several years after the dissolution of his partnership with Whieldon, he devoted his experiments to the production of a cream-coloured, fine earthenware; and by 1763 had invented what he described as 'a species of earthenware for the table, quite new in appearance, covered with a rich and brilliant glaze, bearing sudden alterations of heat and cold, manufactured with ease and expedition, and consequently cheap'. His success with this new ware was striking, particularly since his wares were outstanding in the particular quality he found lacking in the work of his contemporaries — he 'attended to the Elegance of form'. And it is not only the grace, but the variety of his useful wares, which is astonishing. A list would be too long to quote, but his catalogue contains such items as 'Egg Baskets, to keep boiled Eggs hot in water', 'Strawberry Bowls', 'Monteiths for keeping Glasses cool in Water', 'Asparagus Pans', 'Dishes for Water Zootjes' (Dutch fish), and jelly moulds, besides every type of table equipment usually made of silver, such as egg-spoons, mustard-pots, sauce-terrines, and, of course, tea and coffee services complete.

By 1765 Josiah was considering having 'a man in London the greatest part of the year'. His brother John became his first agent there, followed by Mr. William Cox.

A friend reported in the same year that, at a dinner with Lord Gower, 'Wedgwood's potworks were the subject of conversation for some time, the Cream Colour table services in particular . . . his Lordship said that nothing of the sort could exceed them for a fine glaze'. That year too there came the first order from the Royal family. This was for a tea service 'with a gold ground and raised flowers upon it in green'. The order came from an agent in Newcastle-under-Lyme, and Wedgwood thought that it was given to him 'because nobody else would undertake it'. Nor was this surprising, since Queen Charlotte, who ordered it, wanted a type of ware which had not then been made in England. At that time gold in small quantities could be fired on pottery, but large metallic areas were not usual. So Josiah had many technical problems to solve, and referred to them again and again in his letters to John during the

1. Coffee pot and teapot in cauliflower ware. It was ware similar to this which Wedgwood developed when in partnership with Thomas Whieldon from 1754 to 1759.

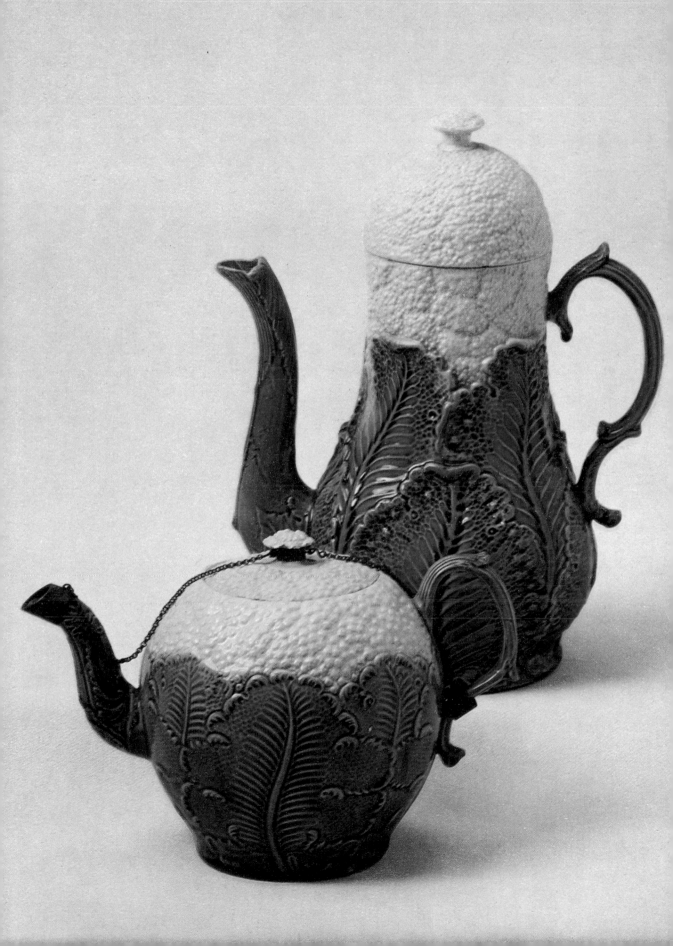

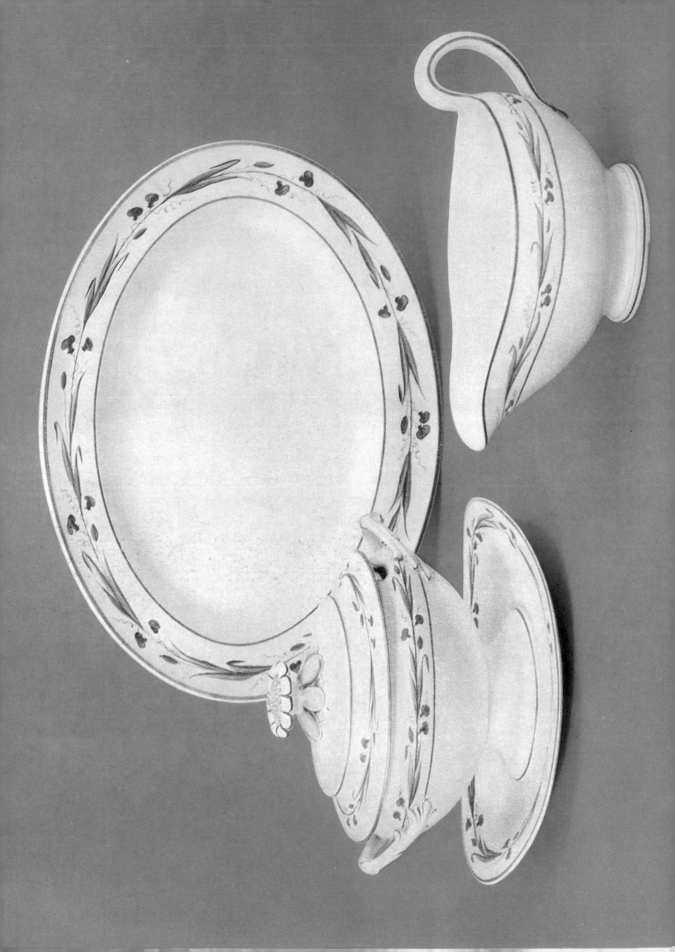

summer of 1765. John also received an urgent message: 'Pray put on *the best suit of clothes you ever had in your life* and take the first opportunity of going to Court.' This was an attempt to find out the Queen's exact wishes from the Palace official who had given the order, so that 'the great Personage they are for would have them perfect'.

The Queen continued to patronize Wedgwood, and her subsequent orders included a set of cream-coloured earthenware. This pleased her so well that, according to Josiah, she commanded that all Wedgwood ware of this nature was thereafter to bear the name Queen's Ware. In 1767 Josiah wrote: 'All hands in the country are not hired but are still coming to me to know when they must begin. . . . The demand for this *said creamcolour*, alias *Queens Ware*, alias *Ivory* still increases. It is really amazing how rapidly the use of it has spread almost over the whole globe, and how universally it is liked.'

Such ware was decorated, much as it is today, by printing or painting with enamel colours or by a combination of both processes. The printing was carried out at first by Sadler and Green of Liverpool, who perfected the process in 1756. Later, the printing was done in Wedgwood's own factory. Hand painting was first done by the widow Warburton in Hot Lane, Burslem, or by Phillips and Greaves in Stoke, but later by Wedgwood's own painters and paintresses in Chelsea. Wedgwood designed many ranges of shapes for his Queen's Ware. Best known, and still made today, were the 'Plain Traditional', the plates with concave rims and the holloware in simple clean lines that seem to match the twentieth century as well as the eighteenth. Others in twentieth century production were 'Catherine', 'Queen's' and 'Shell Edge'.

Dairies could be supplied not only with equipment — settling pans, jugs and bowls — for the dairymaid, but also with tiles for the walls. As early as 1767, Wedgwood asked Bentley to look out for 'a sober Tyle maker among your Potthouses to bring along with you', the Staffordshire men being, we must suppose, what Wedgwood described as 'bibulous'. Ladies were in the habit of visiting the dairy to make a little butter, and would expect to find fresh and neat dairy ware, even before Marie Antoinette at Le Petit Trianon made the whole idea fashionable. A letter from the famous novelist Fanny Burney asks

2. A tureen plate and sauce boat from a dinner set in the 'Convolvulus' pattern, Queen's Ware c. 1780.

B

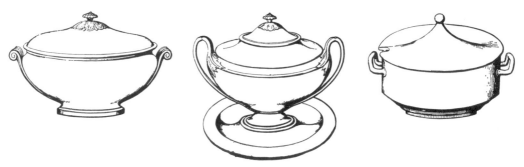

Three Cream Ware designs from an early pattern book engraved by William Blake

her father to get her a small churn. Cream-coloured tiles could be supplied plain, or could be hand-painted or decorated with transfer patterns. The Duchess of Argyll, for instance, had hers printed in a green design by Green of Liverpool. A dairy which survives complete with all its dairy equipment is at Althorp in Northamptonshire. The tiling of the walls is plain, except for hand-painted ivy leaves wreathing the windows and making borders round the walls, and the same ivy pattern decorates the 'cream vases' in which the cream ripened for the butter. Tiles were also supplied for the occasional bathroom, and in a delightful letter in the Wedgwood archives, a dealer negotiating for tiles for the Royal Baths at Brighton begged Josiah Wedgwood II 'Please tow let Me have them as Cheep as yow can For you Must set the out side Price of them so that I may get somethink By them myselph'. He had them for 3/6 a dozen.

The Empress Catherine the Great of Russia was an early customer for cream-coloured ware. A dinner service for some two dozen people, decorated in maroon flowers, was ordered in 1770, and is now displayed in the Palace of Petrodvorets, near Leningrad. However, probably the most famous commission ever executed by Wedgwood in Queen's Ware was the huge combined dinner and dessert service for fifty people, ordered by the Empress for her own use, and completed in 1774. This set consisted ot 952 pieces, hand-painted with English scenes. Mostly, these show landscape gardens of the type made famous by Capability Brown, but there are also wild and romantic scenes, Alnwick castle, Fingal's Cave, or the crags of Derbyshire. Wedgwood scoured the country for suitable illustrations, and had many drawn specially. As large pieces, such as tureens, needed two or more designs, 1,244 different views were required.

No expense was spared, and the financial return on the outlay was extremely small. Catherine the Great's archives show that she paid Wedgwood 16,406 rubles and 43 kopecks, or a little over £2,700, while his expenses have been calculated as being about £2,612. However, as an advertisement the service amply justified itself. It was put on display in Josiah's Greek Street showrooms, was visited by the nobility and also Queen Charlotte, and became the fashionable topic of conversation.

In 1909 the Tsar lent a number of pieces from this service for an exhibition in London, and C. G. Williamson wrote a book on the subject. A few trial pieces are preserved at Barlaston and in other collections, and occasional pieces of the actual service, missing in 1909, appear in the salerooms from time to time. Apart from these, virtually all the service is in Leningrad, where it has astonishingly survived revolution and siege. It is kept in the Hermitage, where some eighty pieces are on display, and a book about it can be bought.

The frog design below appears on almost all the pieces. The palace for which the service was ordered was called Chesmen, but the site had originally been known, in Finnish, as Kekerekeksinsk, or Frog Marsh. Hence the frog which the Empress chose as the symbol of the palace.

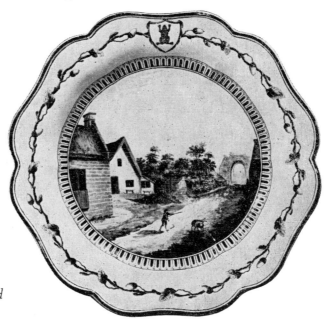

Queen's Ware plate from service supplied to Empress Catherine in 1774. Decorated with a handpainted view of the Island of Anglesey

The Partnership with Bentley

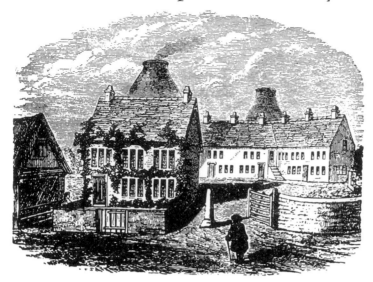

*Ivy House Works,
Burslem*

THE OPENING OF ETRURIA

D URING his early years as a 'master-potter', when he was at the Ivy House
works in Burslem, Josiah made several journeys on horseback to Liverpool
to buy cobalt, to arrange for the printing of his wares by Sadler and Green, and
to see to their shipment to those American colonies in whose later independence
he so greatly rejoiced. On one of these journeys, in 1762, an accident to his
already weakened knee caused him to take to his bed at an inn in Liverpool.
There he was attended by the eminent surgeon, Matthew Turner, who introduced him to 'a man of most courtly manner, evidently possessed of high
intelligence and good taste, and an excellent conversationist'. This was Thomas
Bentley, a Liverpool merchant, who had travelled the Continent, spoke French
and Italian, and had a considerable knowledge of classical and Renaissance art.
From this meeting there sprang a friendship which was much more than a mere
business association, and an almost daily correspondence in which every sorrow
and joy, every difficulty and success, was recorded as frankly as in a private diary.
Wedgwood wrote of Bentley's letters, with characteristic warmth: 'The very

feel of them, even before the seal is broke, cheers my heart and does me good. . . . They inspire me with taste, emulation and everything that is necessary for the production of fine things.' Unfortunately few of them survive. Wedgwood's letters to Bentley, however, have been preserved and reveal the charm of character of the writer, and the details of his daily life, better than any biography; two collections of them have been published. Bentley's death in 1780 was, perhaps, the greatest misfortune in Wedgwood's life.

In 1766 he proposed a partnership with Bentley which was formally agreed to in 1769. The plans for this famous partnership, and for the move to Etruria, were interrupted in May 1768 by an attack of inflammation in Wedgwood's knee. This attack, the last of many, was so serious that the pain and danger of an amputation had to be faced. The risks of an operation at that time, with no anaesthetics and no antiseptics, were of a kind almost impossible to appreciate today; some hint of them can be found in the eighteenth-century regulation of St. Bartholomew's Hospital which obliged every patient, on entry, to deposit nineteen shillings and sixpence for burial dues. These were refunded if the patient was fortunate enough to recover.

Surgical opinion of our own day would suggest that the smallpox from which Wedgwood suffered as a boy left him with an infection which developed into osteomyelitis of the upper end of the tibia, the so-called 'Brodie's abscess'. This would not cause serious incapacity at first, apart from the occasions when he hit or bruised his knee (to one of which, as we have seen, he owed his introduction to Bentley). But in the course of time, the bone thickening which developed would disable the joint completely, making an operation inevitable. The amputation was successfully carried out in 1768 by his surgeon Mr. Bent of Newcastle. The patient made a rapid recovery, thanks to the assiduous care of his wife and the companionship of Bentley, who stayed with him until all danger was over. Wedgwood's health, which had never been good, improved from that time.

Wedgwood had a wooden leg made by a Mr. Addison, of Long Acre, who made 'lay figures for artists'. The excellent naturalistic effect of this leg, clearly displayed in the close-fitting stockings of Georgian dress, can be seen in the Stubbs family group facing page 40.

When the partnership began, Bentley took charge of the London warehouse and showrooms, which were then at Newport Street, St. Martin's Lane, near the fashionable cabinetmakers Chippendale and Vile and Cobb, and later at No. 12 Greek Street, Soho. He also supervised the enamelling department set up in Chelsea, and lived there himself. His time was more than fully occupied with his responsibilities for receiving and despatching orders, collecting debts, ordering raw materials, dealing with the export trade which came through London, providing Wedgwood with designs and borrowed models, providing liaison with artists and modellers, and attending to the *haut ton* who made Wedgwood's showroom one of their social meeting places in London. On May 1st Wedgwood wrote that 'Mrs. Byerley is just return'd from London and brings a strange acc't of their goings on in Newport Street. No getting to the door for Coaches, nor into the rooms for Ladies and Gent'n.'

Bentley and Wedgwood shared the friendship of many eminent men in the worlds of science, art and industry, including Joseph Priestley, James Watt, Matthew Boulton, Erasmus Darwin, Sir Joseph Banks, Sir Joshua Reynolds and George Stubbs.

Meanwhile, Wedgwood had married his third cousin Sarah, only daughter of Richard Wedgwood of Spen Green. The wedding took place at Astbury Parish Church, Cheshire, on January 25th, 1764. Josiah's letters show his wife as a clever, charming and considerate woman, helpful in his business and in his domestic life. She sat in judgment on his new shapes, and assisted in his schemes and experiments. While working on the production of a white earthenware he wrote:

'Sally is my chief helpmate in this as well as in other things, and that she may not be hurried by having too many irons in the fire, as the phrase is, I have ordered the spinning wheel into the lumber room.'

In another letter to Bentley he said:

'Mrs. Wedgwood has tried our new teapots of which we send you one, and gives them her sanctions, as the best and pleasantest in the hand she has ever used. I wish Mrs. Bentley would be so good as to use this pot and favour me with her corrections that we may bring them out as perfect as may be.'

Elsewhere he wrote:

'I speak from experience in Female taste, without which I should have made but a poor figure among my pots, not one of which of any consequence is finished without the approbation of my Sally.'

There were eight children of the marriage, six of whom survived their father — three sons and three daughters. The eldest, Susannah, or 'Sukey', became the mother of Charles Darwin, FRS, the biologist and author of 'The Origin of Species'. The eldest son, John, was a founder of the Royal Horticultural Society; the second son, Josiah, inherited the pottery; and the third, Thomas, became famous after his death as one of the inventors of photography.

At the time of his marriage Wedgwood had already accumulated a modest capital from the profits of his small Burslem Works. This, added to his wife's dowry, enabled him to expand his business considerably. In 1766 he bought for £3,000 the Ridge House Estate, between Hanley and Newcastle-under-Lyme. There he built a new house and splendid new factory, which he named Etruria, in honour of the ancient state in Italy whose arts, particularly pottery, were being rediscovered in his time, and were a source of inspiration to artists and craftsmen. Etruria was opened on June 13th, 1769, and six vases were made to commemorate the event. Wedgwood threw and turned them, while Bentley operated the wheel. They were painted with red classical figures on a black clay,

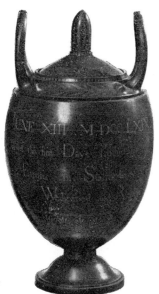

A 'First Day's' Vase

in imitation of the Greek vases found in Etruscan tombs, and were inscribed
'Artes Etruriae Renascuntur' — the arts of Etruria are reborn. Two of these
vases are preserved in the Wedgwood museum at Barlaston. They are generally
known as the 'First Day's' vases.

The family moved to Etruria Hall in November 1769. On that day Josiah
wrote, 'Tonight we are to sup 120 of our workmen in the Town Hall, Burslem.'

Wedgwood's devotion to the Etruria of the past occasionally produced
difficulties for him in the Etruria of the present. In the Wedgwood museum
there is a letter, dated 1787, and sent to him by a firm in Brescia. They apolo-
gize for the delay in sending a bill of exchange, saying that they had made a
previous attempt to send it to Etruria, but that the Director of the Posts at
Mantua had returned it to them, with a covering note saying that though the
letter had been circulated for a considerable time, it had been impossible to
find any place called Etruria. Presumably the postmaster had been misled by
the Italian sound of the address, and had sent it on a tour of central Italy. The
firm's second letter was addressed to London, and arrived there safely.

The old Bell Works at Burslem continued to produce 'useful wares' under
the management of his cousin Thomas, whom Josiah had taken into partnership
for this branch of manufacture in 1766. At first only ornamental pieces were
made at Etruria, but in 1773–4 all production was transferred there and the
Bell Works was closed.

3. An 'encaustic' vase in Black Basalt depicting Penelope with the Bow of Ulysses.

OVERLEAF

4. Black Basalt candlestick in the form of a crouching gryphon, originally one of a pair, first
introduced about 1775. Designed by Sir William Chambers.

5. Two neo-classical vases in marbled clay in imitation of agate. The one in the foreground is
shape number 1 in the book of vase shapes.

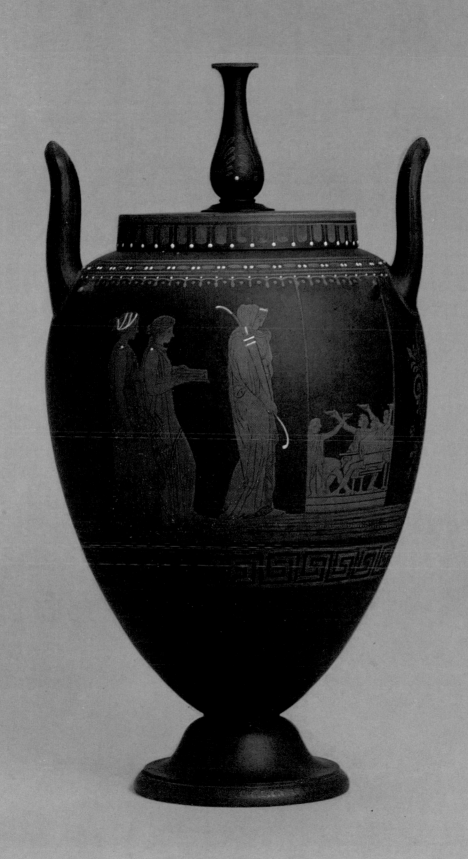

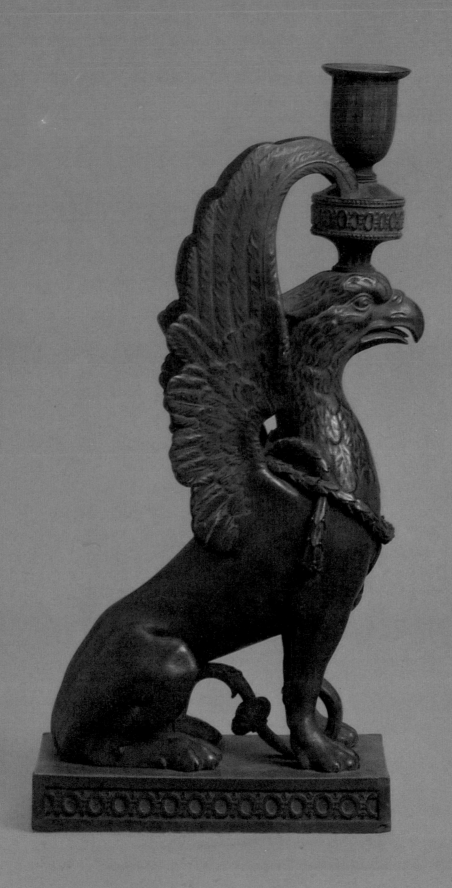

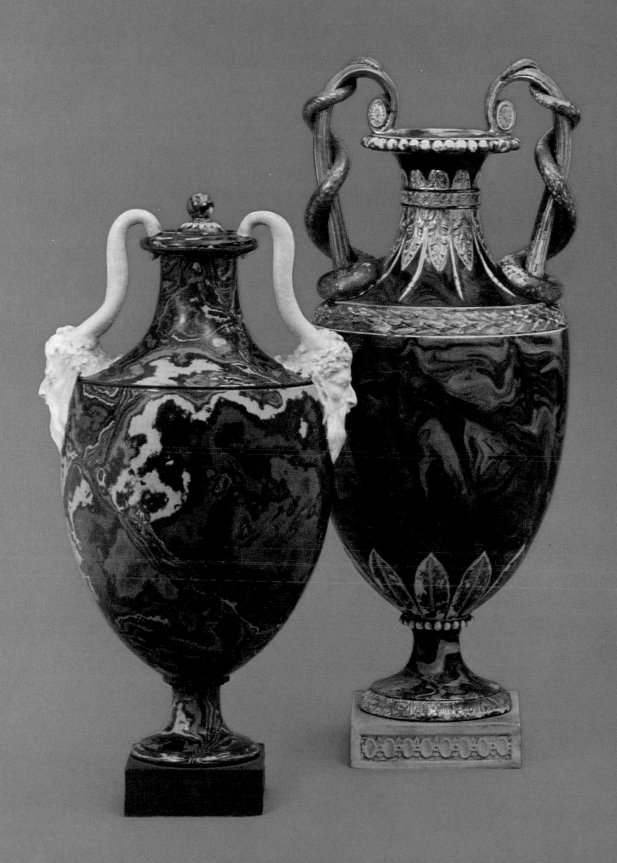

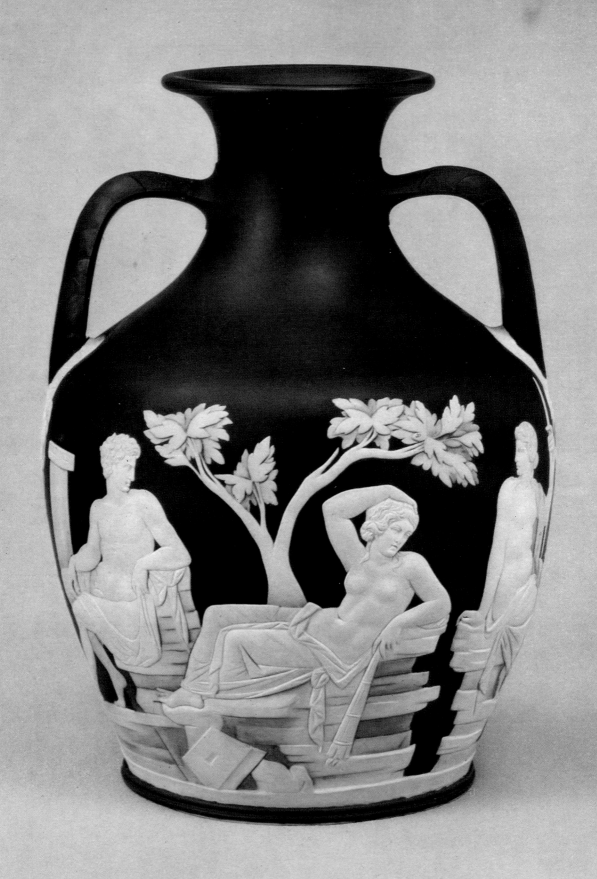

The Invention of Jasper

THE first ornamental ware to be developed by Wedgwood was 'Black Basalt'. It was a refinement of a cruder material known to Staffordshire potters as 'Egyptian Black'. This new black was richer in hue, finer in grain, and smoother in texture than any previously made. Josiah used it both for 'useful' ware and for large relief plaques, vases, busts, medallions, seals and small intaglios. It was also the background on which he executed classical encaustic paintings from a special palette of enamel colours. When these were fired the surface became matt, and closely resembled that of the Greek and Etruscan vases.

In 1773, Wedgwood wrote of his wares:

'The Agate, the Green and other coloured glazes have had their day, and done pretty well, and are certain of a resurrection soon. . . . The Cream Colour is of a superior class, and I trust has not yet run its race by many degrees. The Black is sterling and will last forever.'

The last two prophecies have proved correct. Wedgwood's cream-coloured Queen's Ware is still one of the firm's important products, and Black Basalt remains popular throughout widespread markets.

Jasper, the most famous of Josiah's inventions, appeared first in 1774, and was the result of many experiments. Thousands of his trial pieces have been preserved; yet he himself regretted that he had not kept his earlier ones. Jasper is an unglazed vitreous fine stoneware. It has been made in several shades of blue, in green, lilac, yellow, maroon, black or white; and sometimes one piece combines three or more of these colours. Some of the finest examples of Jasper were made of one coloured body 'dipped' in another colour, and the edges polished and bevelled so that the base colour showed through. The white classical reliefs on a coloured ground are too well known to need description; they are still made today from moulds made from the originals.

Wedgwood prized Jasper above all his productions. He knew the labour of

6. Wedgwood's Portland Vase. This is the 'Hope' copy bought by the antiquarian and collector Thomas Hope in 1793.

its invention and the difficulty of its manufacture. Connoisseurs of pottery since his day have valued it both as a technical triumph and as an ornament perfect of its kind.

The greatest need at the time was for good modellers and designers. William Hackwood, one of the most skilled, had been engaged in 1769. Although six others were employed in 1775, Wedgwood wrote 'we want half a dozen Hackwoods'. In the same year Bentley secured the services of John Flaxman, then only twenty years of age. Among other artists who worked for Wedgwood were James Tassie, Lady Templetown, Joseph Wright, Joachim Smith and George Stubbs, whose portraits of Josiah, his family, his wife and her father are famous. Several of these portraits, and of Stubbs' rural scenes, were painted on large earthenware plaques in ceramic colours which were afterwards fired. Large flat surfaces are extremely difficult to produce in pottery and Josiah must have overcome considerable technical difficulties in enabling Stubbs to paint these pictures, several of which can be seen at the Wedgwood Museum at Barlaston, the Lady Lever Art Gallery, Port Sunlight, the Walker Art Gallery, Liverpool, the Tate Gallery and the National Portrait Gallery, London.

The most outstanding of all Jasper pieces is Wedgwood's replica of the Barberini or Portland Vase. This vase (now in the British Museum) was made in classical times, probably about A.D. 50, and quite possibly in Alexandria, where the most skilled glassmakers of the Roman world were congregated. It is made of deep blue glass, so dark in tone as to appear black and opaque. On this blue background a casing of opaque white glass was put, and then the white layer was carved into figures in shallow relief, leaving the background exposed in many places, a technique requiring extreme skill.

The first documentary evidence about it shows it to have been in the possession of the Barberini family, in Italy, in the early seventeenth century. Wedgwood's friend, Sir William Hamilton, bought it when he was Ambassador to the Kingdom of Naples, and later sold it to the Duchess of Portland. Her son, the Duke, bought the vase at her death, and, when he heard that Josiah wished to make a copy, generously lent it to him.

After years of experiment Wedgwood succeeded in reproducing the colour and surface texture. When, in 1790, he presented his first replica for criticism, it received the approbation of Sir William Hamilton and an appreciation from Sir Joshua Reynolds, President of the Royal Academy, who wrote: 'I can venture to declare it a correct and faithful imitation, both in regard to the general effect, and the most minute detail of the parts.' The number of copies made is uncertain. However, there is evidence in the note-book of Thomas Byerley, Wedgwood's nephew and later partner, of twenty-eight subscribers, but it is not known how many of them actually received their vases. Records show payment for nine only, including those bought by the Duke of Marlborough, John Sneyd, John Trevor and Thomas Hope of Amsterdam. The prices originally paid for these vases varied from £27 6s. 0d. to £33 12s. 0d.

Hope's copy of the Portland Vase was purchased by the firm in 1950 from Mr. Eustace Calland, together with his unique collection of early Wedgwood.

The Trevor vase, Copy No. 9, was part of the Winthrop bequest to the Fogg Museum in Boston, U.S.A.; a further copy was retained by Josiah himself and now belongs to the Wedgwood Museum at Barlaston.

Another issue was made in 1878. Each of these vases was lapidary polished by John Northwood and fifteen were offered for sale through Messrs. Phillips of Oxford Street, London. The names of the subscribers are unknown. Two of these Northwood vases have been purchased back by the company for special display in museums and exhibitions. One is permanently displayed at the Wedgwood, London headquarters. Further replicas have been made from time to time since then.

In adapting classical designs for his Jasper, Wedgwood was following not only his own inclination but also the best taste of his time. In 1759, when Wedgwood started his own factory, Robert Adam had just begun the series of designs which produced a revolutionary change in fashionable taste from the Palladian and rococo to the neo-classical. Pottery was then predominantly rococo in feeling, but Wedgwood saw the possibilities of interpreting the new ideas in ceramic terms, changing the fashion in this field as much as Adam had changed it in interior decoration. Adam's plaques and medallions in low relief, with white classical figures on a pale-coloured ground, such as can be seen at Mellerstain, Osterley, Harewood or almost any other Adam house, lent themselves particularly well to adaptation for Wedgwood's Jasper. Many Jasper pieces were designed for special decorative purposes, to decorate walls, chimneypieces or furniture. The oblong plaques, for instance, with friezes of nymphs or goddesses, were designed for chimneypieces. Two of these survive in Adam houses, and many others in buildings by other late eighteenth century architects following the Adam idiom.

Wedgwood and Bentley went to great trouble to obtain the books of Roman decorative details which were the stock in trade of the neo-classical designers, and we can find, for instance, the same motif stretched out across an Adam portico or shrunk to a Wedgwood medallion which will lie on the palm of the hand. The furniture designers who followed Adam's lead were also able to buy Wedgwood plaques adapted to their special needs. Chippendale, in his neo-classical phase, used Wedgwood medallions in a set of chairs, and Sheraton designed furniture to be decorated with plaques which he described as being 'of an exquisite composition . . . to be had, of any figure or on any subject, at Mr. Wedgewood's [sic] near Soho Square'. Bureaux, bookcases and early pianos can be found ornamented with Wedgwood plaques, and the clock-making Vulliamy family used them extensively. Vases and ornaments in the classical taste were designed at Etruria to add the last touches to neo-classical interiors. The large sets of vases and *garnitures de cheminée* were not perfected until after Bentley's death, but were made in considerable quantities from the 1780's until the end of the century. Where these have been allowed to remain in their proper places, and have not been shut away in display cases, it can be seen how important is the part they play in the exquisite harmony of the Adam style. Customers were prepared to pay high prices for them. The Jasper vase bought in the 1780's for Audley End, and still displayed there, cost £21.

Wedgwood would not have called himself an artist, yet part of his greatness as a man and as a potter lay in his appreciation of the value of the contribution which art can make to industry and in his success in securing the services of the leading painters and sculptors of his day. Furthermore, he was an artist in his own material; he had an appreciation of shape and understood the importance of restraint in design and ornament. The graceful outlines of his Queen's Ware and his simple border decorations, evolved by his own modellers and painters, are even more highly appreciated now than they were in his own life-time.

Canals, Clay and Causes

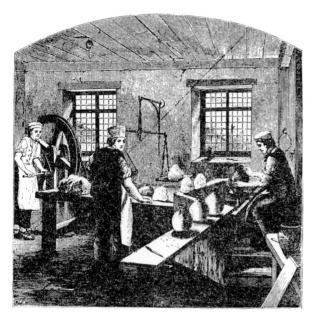

Throwing Room at Etruria
c. 1790

THE difficulties of transport in the district in the middle of the eighteenth century have already been mentioned. Burslem for example had no road; and Arthur Young, after a brief experience of North Staffordshire lanes, wrote: 'Let me persuade all travellers to avoid this terrible country!' No great expansion of commerce could take place in such conditions.

The energetic steps which Wedgwood took to secure better facilities brought him prominently before the public. In 1762 he and others petitioned for a new turn-pike road through Burslem to join that from London to Liverpool. This extract from the petition shows the extent to which the pottery trade had already grown since the beginning of the century.

'In Burslem and its neighbourhood are near 500 separate potteries for making various kinds of stone and earthenware, which find constant employment and support for near 7,000 people. The ware of these potteries is exported in vast quantities from London, Bristol, Liverpool, Hull, etc., to our several colonies in America and the West Indies, as well as to almost every port of Europe. . . .

Many thousand tons of shipping are employed in carrying materials for the Burslem ware; and as much salt is consumed in glazing one species of it as pays annually near £5,000 duty to Government. . . . The trade flourishes so much as to have increased two-thirds within the last 14 years.'

Even if allowance is made for some exaggeration, natural in a petition, the difference between this description and that already quoted of the industry fifty years earlier — when there were only some sixty potteries with a trade of less than £10,000 a year — is very striking. It is even more remarkable that this expansion had taken place, although raw materials and finished products had to be carried between port and factory by river and pack-horse.

Owing to the opposition of vested interests, the petition was only partly successful, and the road was terminated at Stoke instead of Newcastle.

Another turn-pike road was projected in 1765. Of this Wedgwood wrote to his brother John in London: '£2,000 is wanting for this road. My uncles Thomas and John (of the Big House) have, I am quite serious, at the first asking subscribed . . . *five hundred pounds*. I have done the like, intending 2 or 300 of it for you and if you choose any more you must let me know in time.' Two years previously wagons and carts had first appeared in the district.

The Duke of Bridgewater was at this time developing his estates in Cheshire by means of the now famous Bridgewater Canal — the first of its kind. James Brindley, the self-taught engineer, was in charge. He was already well known in North Staffordshire as he had erected a windmill near Burslem for grinding calcined flint for a pottery belonging to Josiah's uncle, John Wedgwood. He had then made a preliminary survey for a canal to connect the rivers Trent and Mersey. As a result of the success of the Bridgewater Canal this second project was revived in 1765 and an association was formed to obtain the necessary parliamentary powers for canal construction. For a year Wedgwood was busy soliciting help and combating the opposition of rival interests. He and Bentley issued pamphlets explaining the advantages of the scheme. At last, in May 1766, the necessary Bill was passed by Parliament and a committee was formed to carry out the work. Brindley was appointed Surveyor General at a salary of £200 per annum. Wedgwood was elected Honorary Treasurer, bearing his own expenses. He had subscribed £1,000 in shares towards the cost of the scheme and had given a security of £10,000 when elected Treasurer. On July 26th, 1766, he cut the first sod at Brownhills, between Burslem and Tunstall, before a great concourse of people. This was a remarkable honour for a business man still in his thirties. It is recorded that an ox was roasted whole on that day to commemorate the occasion.

This canal, which was completed in 1777 was a great engineering triumph. It linked two rivers across the breadth of the Midlands of England — a distance of 93 miles. There were 75 locks. At its highest point the canal culminated in a tunnel nearly 3,000 yards long. The result was a reduction in transport costs from 10d. to 1½d. per ton mile. Furthermore it proved a highly profitable venture; in 1824 £100 of stock was quoted at £2,200 and the dividend was 75 per cent. The canal passed through the Wedgwood estate at Etruria and a branch was brought to the works itself.

The artist in Josiah wanted the canal to proceed in graceful curves, and he wrote of the Clerk of the Works 'I could not prevail upon that Vandal to give me one line of grace — he must go the nearest and best way or Mr. Brindley would go mad!' Being a man of the later eighteenth century, and an admirer of the large-scale landscape gardening of Capability Brown, Wedgwood assumed quite naturally that the canal, though put there for convenience, could easily be made into a feature of the landscape. Today, of course, the assumption is

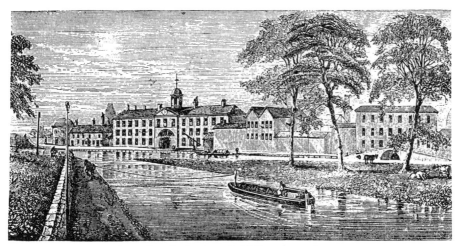

Canalside view of old Etruria works

made all too easily that industrial constructions, however useful, will automatically make a desolation of the scenery, although the present Wedgwood factory provides excellent evidence to the contrary.

Mining underneath Etruria caused the works to subside below the level of the canal, and it has been demolished. Nevertheless, until the factory at Etruria was abandoned, the canal provided the cheapest means of transporting clays and flints from Runcorn, near Liverpool, whither they were conveyed by sea from Devon, Cornwall and the north coast of France.

Flints and white clays from Devon had been introduced into the manufacture of earthenware by Astbury in the early part of the century. In 1756 Cookworthy discovered pure white china clay and china stone in Cornwall and in 1768 he took out a patent to use them for the manufacture of porcelain. His project was not successful and five years later he sold the patent to Richard Champion. The latter attempted to obtain an extension of his sole right for a further seven years.

In the meantime these materials had become standard ingredients of Queen's Ware and of white earthenware generally. Wedgwood naturally played an important part in opposing the extension of Champion's monopoly in 1775. He had been criticized for trying to prevent a struggling inventor from obtaining his due reward. But Champion was not the discoverer of china stone and its uses. Far from attempting to stop an honest man from profiting from the results of his labours, Wedgwood (and other potters) fought to free the supply of a natural product to all would-be consumers. Full justice was done when Champion was allowed the patent for the manufacture of *porcelain*, all other potters were permitted to use this stone for the making of earthenware only.

Wedgwood foresaw the possibility of colonial competition. In a letter of the mid-sixties, he wrote that 'this trade to the colonies we are apprehensive of losing in a few years, as they have set on foot some pott works there already and have at this time an agent amongst us hiring a number of our hands for establishing a new pott works in South Carolina, having got one of our insolvent Master Potters there to conduct them. They have every material there, equal if not superior to our own, for carrying on that manufacture'. Mr. Bartlem was the Master Potter, who was there by 1766. He took his tendency to insolvency across the Atlantic with him, and the works were unsuccessful.

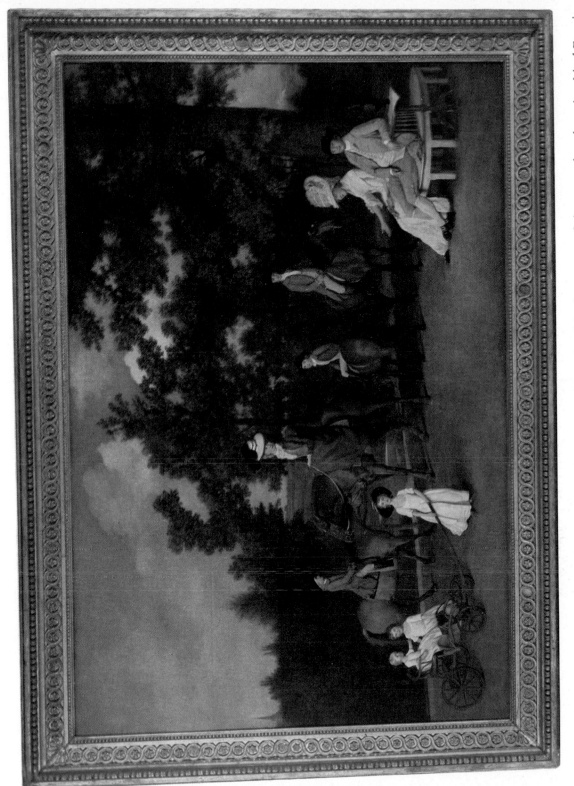

7. The Wedgwood Family in 1780, a portrait in oils by George Stubbs painted in the summer of that year when the artist visited Etruria.

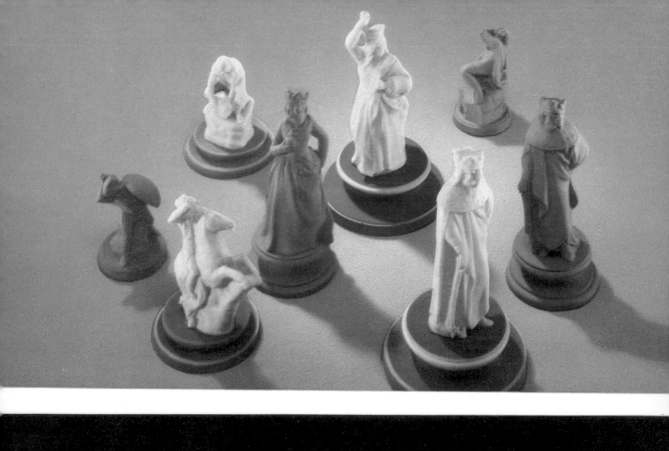
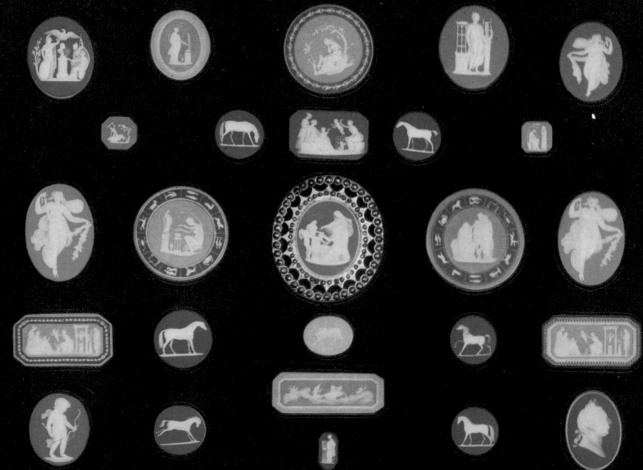

In 1768 Wedgwood sent Thomas Griffiths to America to find and purchase the white clay of the Carolinas from the Cherokee Indian nation. At a cost of £500, Griffiths obtained about five tons of the clay, which was transported with great difficulty to the coast. On June 12th, 1950, a historical marker was placed on Highway 28, five miles north of Franklin, North Carolina, to indicate the position of the pit, and to commemorate this use of the Cherokee clay.

In 1788 Wedgwood again used clay from overseas. This time it was obtained for him by Sir Joseph Banks, P.R.S., through Governor Phillip of New South Wales. From this clay William Hackwood modelled a medallion, after a design by Henry Webber, to commemorate the landing of the Settlers at Sydney Cove. The figures it represents — Hope, attended by Peace, Art and Labour — were suitably immortalized in Erasmus Darwin's poem 'The Botanic Garden'. Medallions were also struck of Sir Joseph and Lady Banks, Captain Cook and Dr. Solander, friends of Wedgwood, whose names are so closely associated with the early days of Australia.

The use of Cherokee and Australian clays were not isolated occurrences. Wedgwood even tried clay from Canton, and in 1792 wrote that 'I have been for near forty years searching in different parts of the world for earths, stones and minerals, chiefly such as had, or might be brought to have, some relation to the manufacture I am engaged in'.

WEDGWOOD'S LATER YEARS

Bentley's death in 1780 robbed Wedgwood of a dear friend and an ideal partner. For the next ten years he carried on his work alone, but in 1790 he took into partnership his three sons and his sister's son, Thomas Byerley. In 1793 his sons John and Thomas retired and conveyed their shares to their brother Josiah. The name of the firm was therefore, 'Wedgwood & Bentley' from 1769 to 1780, 'Wedgwood' from 1780 to 1790, 'Wedgwood, Sons & Byerley' from 1790 to 1793, and 'Wedgwood & Son & Byerley' from 1793 to 1795.

In 1783 Josiah was elected a Fellow of the Royal Society. A year previously he had read a paper before the Society on a new and ingenious instrument for measuring high temperatures. Five of his papers were published by the Society,

8. Examples of Jasper chessmen from designs by the sculptor John Flaxman, first produced in 1784.
9. A frame of Jasper cameos including six of the 18 horse studies by George Stubbs and a cameo mounted in cut steel, all c. 1790.

three relating to his pyrometer and two to the chemistry of clays. Although he was not a professional chemist — and the science of chemistry was then in its infancy — his scientific knowledge was far in advance of that possessed by other potters. He was well acquainted with the discoveries of his friend, Dr. Joseph Priestley F.R.S. Wedgwood was one of several generous supporters who enabled Priestley to carry out his experiments, and supplied him, and other chemists, with specially made apparatus such as retorts, tubes, pans and the more widely known pestles and mortars. He possessed the scientific mind in an age when that was rare. 'Everything yields to experiment' was his motto. He did his best to convince his workmen that things did not happen without a cause. He was methodical, and his jottings in his 'Commonplace Book' and other note-books indicate that there are few things known to the modern potter which Wedgwood did not discover for himself.

His personality is clearly revealed in his many letters. No one who reads them can fail to be impressed, not only by his energy, but even more by his lovable character and liberal mind. His public and private acts testify to the warmth and generosity of his disposition. He was a great business man, but not a mercenary one. He devoted himself to his work for its intrinsic interest and for the sake of achievement rather than for private gain. 'So far from being afraid of other people getting our patterns,' he wrote to Bentley, 'we should glory in it, throw out all the hints we can and if possible have all the Artists in Europe working after our models. This would be noble and would suit both our dispositions and sentiments much better than all narrow, mercenary, selfish channels. . . . There is nothing relating to business I so much wish for as being released from these degrading selfish chains, these mean selfish fears of other people copying my works.'

He contributed freely to the causes in which he believed, not merely to those which might help his business. In 1760, when he had only been established independently for a year, we find him giving £10 towards a second Free School in Burslem, a contribution equalling that of the richest potters. In 1792, when wealthy, he subscribed £250 to help the people of Poland against the Russian invasion. Although his trade depended much on the patronage of royalty and nobility, he was no sycophant. In 1778, when the American War of Independence was entering its bitterest phase, he supported the American cause. On March 3rd of that year he wrote in a letter to Bentley that he 'blessed his stars and Lord North that America is free' from the iron hand of tyranny. In one of the last letters to his partner he wrote, 'Every member of the State must either have a vote or be a slave.' The same general sentiments were expressed to his son in 1790: 'A real parliamentary reform is what we most stand in need of, and for this I would willingly devote my time, the most precious thing I have to bestow, or anything else by which I could serve so truly noble a cause.'

A year earlier he wrote to Erasmus Darwin, 'I know you will rejoice with me in the glorious revolution which has taken place in France. The politicians tell me that as a manufacturer I shall be ruined if France has her liberty, but I am willing to take my chance in that respect, nor yet do I see that the happiness of one nation includes in it the misery of its next neighbour.' The French Revolution and the war which followed in fact injured Wedgwood's trade and that of his son, but this did not alter their views on political liberty.

These sentiments were shared by Bentley, who, though a Liverpool merchant, denounced the slave trade on which Liverpool then throve. Wedgwood was an ardent supporter of the Anti-Slavery Committee, and a generous subscriber to its funds. Hackwood modelled a cameo which depicted a slave kneeling in

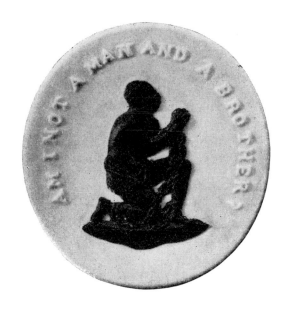

The Slave Medallion designed by Wedgwood and adopted as the seal of the Slave Emancipation Society

chains, with the inscription 'Am I not a man and a brother?' and Wedgwood had thousands of these cameos made, and distributed them free to anyone concerned with anti-slavery propaganda. Clarkson, a fellow member of the Committee, said that he had over five hundred himself, and a letter exists from Benjamin Franklin, who had received a parcel of the medallions for use in the newly independent United States, thanking Wedgwood and saying that he was persuaded that the medallion 'may have an effect equal to that of the best written pamphlet'. These little medallions were mounted as hatpins, buttons, rings, and in many other ways. Clarkson wrote that 'the taste for wearing them became general, and thus fashion, which usually confines itself to worthless things, was seen for once in the honourable office of promoting the cause of justice, humanity and freedom'.

This illustrates Wedgwood's sensitivity to what was topical, and his exceptional ingenuity in commemorating people and events in ceramics. He had portrait medallions made of many of the notabilities of his day, not only members of the Royal family and of the aristocracy, but politicians such as Pitt and Fox, scientists such as Sir William Herschel and Dr. Priestley, explorers such as Captain Cook. Actors included Garrick and Mrs. Siddons, writers Shakespeare and Dr. Johnson and philosophers Voltaire and Rousseau.

Wedgwood's interests in the struggle for liberty in America led him to have portraits made of Washington and Benjamin Franklin. Lawrence Sterne's *Sentimental Journey*, one of the most popular novels of the time, inspired two medallions; and Wedgwood must have been one of the first to use a theme from Goethe's *Sorrows of Werther*, later to become an essential textbook for the Romantic Movement.

This quick reaction to current events can be seen particularly clearly at the time of the French Revolution. The Bastille fell on July 14th, 1789. On the 24th, Wedgwood's son, Josiah II, was writing to his father, 'Do you think it would be proper to get some snuff-box tops with the Duke of Orléans' head on them? You will no doubt have seen in the papers that the French have recovered their liberty and that the Duke is a great favourite with the popular party.' By the 28th the portraits of the Duc d'Orléans, and also of M. Necker the financier, were in production, and Josiah II had turned his mind to a more symbolic piece. 'What do you think', he wrote, 'of a figure of Public Faith at an altar, and France embracing Liberty at the Front?' A rough design for this was ready by the 29th, and Josiah II remarked that 'the figure of Hope in the Botany Bay medal would come in exceedingly well for this figure of Liberty, and the other two would be modelled very soon'. Three versions were made (one following Josiah II's idea of France and Liberty embracing, and two re-using the Hope figure as Liberty), together with the Orléans portrait, and that of another revolutionary leader, Mirabeau.

Wedgwood's correspondence also sheds a pleasant sidelight on his domestic life. Amidst the pressure of all his business activities he found time to take his children to and from school, to ride with them before breakfast, and to give them lessons himself. 'Before breakfast,' he writes, 'we read English together in the newspaper or any book we happen to have in the course of reading . . . with the globe and maps before us.'

In 1790 he partially retired from his more active duties and took longer holidays than before. But his health continued to give anxiety, and after a brief illness, he died on January 3rd, 1795, at the age of 64. His grave is in the churchyard at Stoke, and in the chancel of the adjoining church there is a monument by Flaxman, with the following inscription: 'He converted a rude and inconsiderable manufactory into an elegant Art and an important part of the National Commerce.'

In 1863 the foundation stone of the Wedgwood Memorial Institute in Burslem was laid by Mr. Gladstone, then Chancellor of the Exchequer. In his address he said of Wedgwood, 'He was the greatest man who ever, in any age or in any country, applied himself to the important work of uniting art with industry.'

A more recent tribute to Wedgwood's work by a modern ceramic expert, William Burton, may also be quoted: 'His influence was so powerful, and his personality so dominant, that all other English potters worked on the principles he had laid down, and thus a fresh impulse and a new direction was given to the pottery of England and of the civilized world. He is the only potter of whom it may truly be said that the whole subsequent course of pottery manufacture has been influenced by his individuality, skill and taste.'

The Nineteenth Century

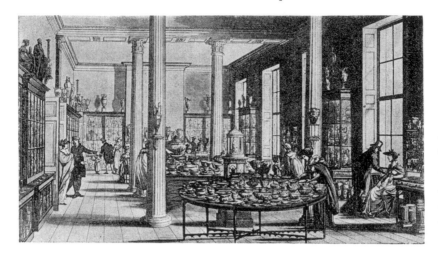

Wedgwood & Byerley's show-room, York Street St. James's, London. Wood engraving from mezzotint of 1809

JOSIAH WEDGWOOD left a large fortune to his widow and six surviving children. His second son, Josiah II (1769–1843) who had been his partner at Etruria since 1790, inherited the works and an estate of 380 acres, but retired to the country in 1795 and left the management of Etruria to his cousin Thomas Byerley. Byerley had taken an active part in the management of the firm during his uncle's lifetime, and together with Josiah II had become a partner. His uncle had taken an interest in him ever since the day in 1763 when he arrived, a literary-minded youth with a trunkful of manuscripts, on Wedgwood's doorstep. Later he tried the stage, but gave it up 'from a conviction of his inability to succeed in any tolerable degree'. 'I do not know', wrote his uncle, 'what we shall do with him, to keep him out of mischief and put him in the way of being of some use in the World.' When still only twenty he went off to America where he became a private tutor. On his return to England in 1775 he settled down as a general assistant to Wedgwood, translating and writing in French, teaching the children and travelling for the firm.

He undertook, with Josiah II, an extended tour of France, Germany and Holland to show the Portland Vase. On the death of Bentley in 1780 he had taken over the management of the London showrooms.

However he was lacking in technical experience and was not competent to administer single-handed a factory of the size and importance of Etruria, probably then the largest pottery in the world, particularly at a time when trading conditions were extremely difficult. In 1804, therefore, he was relieved of his responsibilities at the factory, and went back to his post as manager of the London showrooms, then in York Street, St. James's, until his death in 1810. Josiah II resumed his charge of the works.

The Napoleonic Wars were disastrous for trade with the continent of Europe. To increase business, Josiah II began in 1812 to manufacture bone china. Translucent porcelain had been made by other Staffordshire potters before this, but had not been made by Wedgwood. However, the china he produced seems not to have satisfied Josiah II's exacting standards. As early as 1814, Lieut.-Col. Johann Conrad Fischer, an Engineer of the Swiss Army, records that Josiah II expressed himself in the following remarkable terms: 'Mr. Fischer, I cannot recommend you to buy porcelain from me; as you will return through France, you will find something better, and more beautiful, in Paris; I may abandon altogether the preparation of porcelain,' Josiah explained that France was in possession of far better material for the making of porcelain than was in England. It is not surprising therefore, that when trade revived in 1816, the manufacture of bone china was gradually discontinued, and ceased altogether in 1828. With the return of prosperity, Josiah II devoted the whole of his attention to the making of Queen's Ware and Jasper. The production of bone china was only begun again in 1878, though since then it has been an increasing part of Wedgwood output. A visitor to the present factory would certainly not be given the same advice that Josiah II gave to Colonel Fischer!

Fischer's diary contains a description of the Etruria works which is remarkable both for its thoroughness and understanding. He spent only a morning in the factory, but was able, at the end of it, to give accurate details of the machinery in use and the various techniques employed. It appears that he had visited potteries elsewhere, and could compare Wedgwood's practice with that usual in other countries. He found much that was new to him.

He describes in detail the ingenious method by which the potters' wheels, driven mechanically, could be made to revolve fast or slowly at will. Though it was now powered by steam, the machinery seems to have been based on the wheel shown in the illustration on page 37, and installed by Josiah I nearly thirty years before.

Many of the new devices he noticed are still in use in the Wedgwood factory of today. He was struck by the use of sand for bedding the ware in the kiln, to minimize distortion in the firing. He explained the method of making a plate by first preparing a clay 'bat' on a revolving wheel, and then shaping it on a plaster jig formed to the contour of the top of the plate. He noticed the device (the 'dod' machine) which extruded clay strips of any desired section for handles, basket-work, and so on. All of these things can be seen in the later twentieth century.

In the decorating section he studied the method of making transfers from engraved copper plates, describing what is substantially the method used today. It is interesting that he ascribed the invention of transfer printing, not to Sadler and Green, of Liverpool, but to Adam Spengler in Switzerland. But Spengler, according to Fischer, invented the process in 1761, and Sadler and Green were already printing by the mid seventeen-fifties; it seems that Spengler either copied, or found out for himself, a technique already in use in England.

Fischer was as much impressed by the factory organization as by the new devices. 'I was filled with wonder', he says, 'by the simplicity of the procedure and the clever apportioning of the work.' Already, by the beginning of the nineteenth century, the Wedgwoods, father and son, had recognized and solved problems of large-scale production, though manufacture on this scale was something entirely new in England. Fischer recognized this. 'As the time for departure approached,' he said, 'I took leave of this man whose father, an ordinary Staffordshire potter, founded an earthenware factory whose articles, because of their merit, will be sent to all quarters of the globe, and where at present his son is doing everything possible to increase the already established reputation.'

In the following year a dinner service was ordered by the Government at the request of the Prince Regent for the use of the ex-Emperor Napoleon whilst in captivity on St. Helena. A modern version of this design, known as Napoleon Ivy, is manufactured today.

A Frenchman, M. Faujas de Saint Fond, who visited Staffordshire in 1816 has written of its earthenware: 'Its excellent workmanship, its solidity, the advantage which it possesses of sustaining the action of fire, its fine glaze impenetrable to acids, the beauty and convenience of its form, and the cheapness of its price have given rise to a commerce so active and universal that in traveling from Paris to St. Petersburg, from Amsterdam to the farthest part of Sweden, and from Dunkirk to the extremity of the South of France, one is served at every inn with English ware. France, Portugal and Italy are supplied, and vessels are loaded with it for the East and West Indies and the continent of America.'

For the first twelve years of the nineteenth century, Josiah II was helped by his brother John. During this period, some of the designs, probably under John's influence, were taken from botanical illustrations. The most famous of these is the 'Water Lily' pattern, of which Dr. Darwin, father of Charles and brother-in-law of Josiah II, ordered a set in 1808, printed in brown and gold. The same design could also be had in underglaze blue, and a number of other designs were also printed by this technique. The Prince Regent, at the Pavilion in Brighton, had revived the fashion for chinoiserie, and a number of oriental designs were evolved for earthenware and also for bone china.

By 1828 trade was again depressed. The London showrooms were abandoned, and the stock of ware, old moulds and models was sold for £16,000. This sale was regrettable since it lost to the firm many pieces of historical interest.

For this error, and also for his absence from the factory for ten years after his father's death, Josiah Wedgwood II has been criticized. Nevertheless, he carried on the tradition of good relationship with his employees, and gave more than customary consideration for their well-being in times of general depression. In return, when he stood for Parliament, his workmen subscribed to a fund for his election expenses. Yet, though his letters to his father discussing labour relations and the day-to-day running of the factory make interesting reading, he seems to have lacked his father's capacity for getting on friendly terms immediately with anyone from a freed slave to a marquess. When he was only twenty-two and Byerley, the London manager, was ill, Josiah II wrote to his father offering to take over the management of the London showrooms 'and to do whatever other business I could, except attending to the rooms any farther than waiting on some particular people, for I have too long had the habit of looking upon myself as the equal of everybody to bear the haughty manners of those who come into a shop'. Of his manner in later years, Sidney Smith made a neat, if acid, summary: 'Wedgwood is an excellent man; it is a pity that he hates his friends.' Charles Darwin, FRS, his nephew and son-in-law, described his austere character with more sympathy. In his autobiography, Darwin wrote that 'He was the very type of an upright man, with the clearest judgment. I do not believe that any power on earth could make him swerve an inch from what he considered the right course'.

The great scientist also relates how his own father, Dr. R. W. Darwin, FRS, who had destined him for the Church, had raised objections to his wish to take part in the famous voyage of *The Beagle*. Dr. Darwin was, however, persuaded to change his mind as a result of the personal intervention of his brother-in-law, Josiah Wedgwood II. It was during this voyage that the young Darwin formulated his revolutionary ideas on evolution, which later resulted in his great work '*The Origin of Species*'.

Josiah II unbent only with his brother Tom, whom he held in the deepest affection. Indeed, he wrote to his wife that 'I have been sometimes afraid that you might think I take from you to give to him'. Tom, however, seems to have inherited in his character some of the fascination of Josiah I. Wordsworth spoke of him in the terms he usually reserved for Nature — 'His calm and dignified manner, united with his tall person and beautiful face, produced in me an impression of sublimity beyond what I ever experienced from the appearance of any human being.' Tom's early death, at the age of 33, was a great blow to Josiah II.

Tom inherited his father's interest in chemical experiments, and as already mentioned was one of the inventors of photography. He tried to use the action of light on silver salts, discovered nearly a century before by the German scientist, Schulze, for the purpose of making photographic pictures. He used the *camera obscura*, but unfortunately silver nitrate was not sensitive enough. However he did succeed in reproducing the image of leaves, insects, etc., on sensitized leather, making what are now called photograms; but neither he nor his scientist friend, Sir Humphry Davy, with whom he was working closely, was able to solve the problem of fixing the image, which slowly faded away when exposed to the light. Tom therefore kept a stock of his 'experiments' in a dark room which he showed to his friends. Helmut Gernsheim said that Wedgwood first had the idea of photography and demonstrated its possibility. A letter written at Lacock Abbey on February 13th, 1839, by Fox Talbot, who was probably the first man to produce photographs comparable to those of today, referred to Wedgwood's work on this subject.

Josiah and his brother Thomas are also remembered for their generous support of the poet and philosopher, Samuel Taylor Coleridge.

After the passage of the Great Reform Bill in 1832 Josiah was elected Member of Parliament for Stoke-on-Trent as a Whig, and voted for the repeal of the Corn Laws. He died in 1843.

Josiah III (1795–1880) entered the business in 1823 but retired in 1842. Thenceforth the third son, Francis (1800–88), who had been admitted as a partner in 1827, carried on the management. The fourth son, Hensleigh, who achieved fame as an etymologist, was never associated directly with the firm.

The period of 1840–80 was one of modernization. Many new scientific labour-saving devices were introduced — the filter-press for drying clay, blungers for mixing and pug-mills for preparing it. Solid Jasper was reintroduced after an interval of seventy years. This was a Jasper in which the background colour extended right through the body of the clay, instead of being a thin 'slip' coating on the surface. Further coloured bodies were also developed in earthenware, among them 'Celadon' (pale grey-green), 'Cane' and 'Lavender'. 'Parian Ware', a fine white body giving something of the effect of marble, was also much in demand during this mid-Victorian period.

Josiah I was greatly admired at this time, but more as a personality and an innovator than for his influence on the design of his times. Eliza Meteyard wrote her monumental *Life of Josiah Wedgwood* in 1865–66; another biography was written by Llewellyn Jewitt in the same year, and later Samuel Smiles took Wedgwood as the classic example of his theories of Self-Help. But the taste of the sixties and seventies was for elaboration — complication of form, richness of decoration, including plenty of gold and a profusion of bright colours. The Wedgwood traditions of austere elegance of shape and sparing decoration had to be abandoned for the time being. There was, however, one artist who stood apart from the tendencies of his time. Emile Lessore began to work for Wedgwood in 1858, and painted his own designs himself, directly on to specially thrown pieces. He wrote: 'I was engaged by Mr. Wedgwood, free to name my own conditions, to choose my own workmen, my own materials. Mr. Wedgwood reposed confidence in me. I did not abuse it. I have drawn and coloured 4,000 pieces in two years.' In the ceramic field of his day he was unique, at a time when the designer and craftsman had drifted apart; and it is interesting that his appointment with Wedgwood antedates by three years the formation of William Morris's company of artist-craftsmen in 1861, the date usually given in art histories as marking the beginning of the modern conception of applied design. Lessore had to leave England on account of his health in 1863, but he continued to do work for Wedgwood until his death in 1875.

Lessore, as a craftsman, could only make a very limited number of individual pieces. He had little influence on the bulk of the factory's production, for which a number of new decorative techniques were evolved about this time. Photographic ornament was tried, with odd results, and lithography was first attempted in 1863. At that time, however, the aim of lithography was to make as close an imitation of oil painting as possible, so that lithographic decoration lacked the freedom and individuality which make it one of the most useful decorative techniques of our day. Bone china manufacture was revived in 1878 and has been carried on with increasing success ever since. The fortunes of the firm allowed the reopening of the London showrooms in 1875.

Parallel to these changes in the field of design were others in the field of organization. This was the age of factory legislation and the growth of the Trades Unions. Relations between organized labour and management developed amicably and there has never been a strike in the Wedgwood factory.

The fourth generation of Wedgwoods began to join the firm in 1870. The first was Godfrey (1833–1905). He was followed by Clement (1840–89) and Lawrence (1844–1913).

Francis Wedgwood died in 1888. For twenty-seven years, from 1843–70, he alone controlled the factory. Members of the firm who knew him remembered him as an imposing man of forceful personality. He was a radical and is reputed to have bought land in different parts of the country in order to have more votes to support the Great Reform Bill. In 1854 he had entertained at his home in Barlaston the Hungarian liberal revolutionary, Kossuth, during his speech-making tour of England in aid of his oppressed compatriots.

From the days of Josiah Wedgwood I, the active managers had always been the owners of the business which, since 1827, had been known as Josiah Wedgwood & Sons. However, with the company law reforms of the later nineteenth century, it became necessary, in 1895, to change the firm from a partnership to a limited liability company.

From 1884 the fifth generation began to come in. The first was Cecil (1863–1916), thereafter Francis Hamilton (1867–1930) and Kennard Lawrence (1873–1950).

The Twentieth Century

IN 1902 John E. Goodwin became art director and introduced a number of new shapes for Queen's Ware, including Edme, Wellesley and Patrician based on Georgian originals. Under the guidance of Alfred and Louise Powell, both distinguished ceramic artists, a school of hand painting was established. Powder colour decoration, a revival of the old Chinese method of stippling with a sponge, was introduced and is still used today for some of the more richly decorated patterns.

By the beginning of the twentieth century, interest in late eighteenth century design had revived once more, and early Wedgwood ware was prized by collectors. Many original trials, moulds, and finished pieces from the earliest days of the factory still existed at Etruria, despite Josiah II's sales, and in 1905 these were collected to form the nucleus of the Wedgwood Museum which was opened in 1906. The collection, which is now considered to be the most comprehensive in the world, includes the Experiment, 'Commonplace' and Pattern books of Josiah Wedgwood, FRS, letters to him from leading artists, scientists and philosophers of his day, with all of whom he corresponded on equal terms, and most of his letters to his partner Bentley. In 1950 the company's collection of early Wedgwood was further increased by the purchase from Mr. Eustace Calland of the finest collection of Wedgwood in private hands. As mentioned on page 35 it included the Portland Vase which belonged to Thomas Hope and since 1968 has housed the Wedgwood Family picture by George Stubbs, bequeathed to the Museum trust by Miss Phoebe Wedgwood. The work of maintaining and supervising the museum, which now covers all phases of the history of Wedgwood, requires the full-time attention of a curator. In 1975, the company built a new museum and picture gallery, within the factory as part of a major reorganization of amenities for the 50,000 people who visit Barlaston each year.

As will have been seen, the Wedgwood and Darwin families were closely connected, and have produced between them a number of eminent people, in many walks of life, during the last 150 years, including the composer Dr. Ralph

Vaughan Williams, OM, who was a direct descendant of Josiah I. Dr. Vaughan Williams was interested in the firm, and at the time of his death was about to compose a cantata, based on a text written by his wife, for the bicentenary in 1959. In 1944, he presented to the Wedgwood Museum a number of family portraits, including works by Romney, Reynolds and Stubbs. For some years these paintings hung at Leith Hill Place, near Dorking, Surrey, a house which originally belonged to Josiah III and which passed to the family of Dr. Vaughan Williams; he later presented it to the National Trust.

DEVELOPMENTS IN AMERICA

From the earliest days, Josiah I was interested in trade with what were then the American colonies, sending out his wares to them from Liverpool. We have seen that as early as the seventeen-sixties he was worried by the possibility of competition from potteries established on American soil and using the excellent raw materials available there. The possibility did not materialise in his day, although today America produces much pottery of good quality. In 1906 the firm took a step of which its founder would have approved, and opened a branch sales office in New York under Kennard Wedgwood. It was incorporated as an American company in 1920. Kennard showed typical Wedgwood energy and resourcefulness, and from 1930 there was a remarkable expansion of trade with the U.S.A. and Canada. During the last sixty years, sales to North America have increased vastly in volume, and at present a large proportion of the company's exports are sold in the North American continent. During the period of President Theodore Roosevelt, a china service of 1,282 pieces was supplied for the White House.

A feature of the American trade is the production of specially commissioned commemorative ware. Such pieces were a speciality of the first Josiah, and his portrait medallions included many Americans: John Paul Jones, Franklin and Washington among them. He was also always prepared to undertake special commissions for particular customers. This type of production lapsed during the nineteenth century, but towards the end of the century a series of historical tile calendars were made which had a great success on the American market.

This led to a unique commemorative ware business, which has produced several thousand special engravings to commemorate, mostly in America, anniversaries, places and historical events.

The first Josiah Wedgwood who was said 'to have changed the eating habits of a nation' kept himself informed about the tastes in other countries. He read, for instance, the letters from Turkey by Lady Mary Wortley Montagu, to discover how he might furnish Turkish interiors with his own ware. He would have been interested to observe the problems and opportunities of the Wedgwood designer of today in producing patterns for tableware appropriate to the many different eating habits and etiquettes of the nations which buy Wedgwood ware.

DEVELOPMENTS AT HOME

In 1916 Major Cecil Wedgwood, DSO, was killed while leading the 8th Battalion of the North Staffordshire Regiment into action at La Boiselle during the battle of the Somme. He had been first Mayor of Stoke-on-Trent, the federation of the six pottery towns. He was succeeded as chairman and managing director by his cousin, Francis Hamilton ('Frank') Wedgwood.

After World War I, there was a renaissance in design, accompanied by many technical improvements. From 1918 Wedgwood played a leading part in introducing the oil-fired tunnel oven into the industry. Much modernization was carried out and methods of production improved. Large and up-to-date decorating shops were built.

The bicentenary of the birth of Josiah I was celebrated in 1930. The celebrations were opened by H.R.H. Princess Mary, and were attended by representatives of the pottery trade from all over the world. They came to pay tribute to the memory of the great potter. Workers from the industry gave a pageant portraying the history of the district. That part which depicted the life and times of Josiah I was presented by members of the Wedgwood family and 700 workers from Etruria, under the direction of Hensleigh Wedgwood.

10. A solid blue Jasper solitaire tea set with reliefs modelled by William Hackwood from designs by Lady Templetown c. 1785.

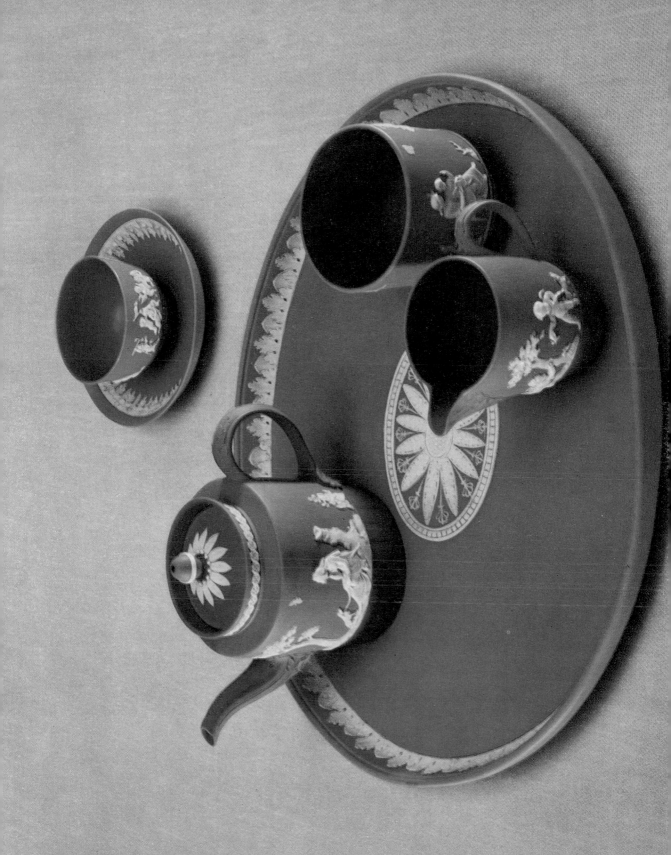

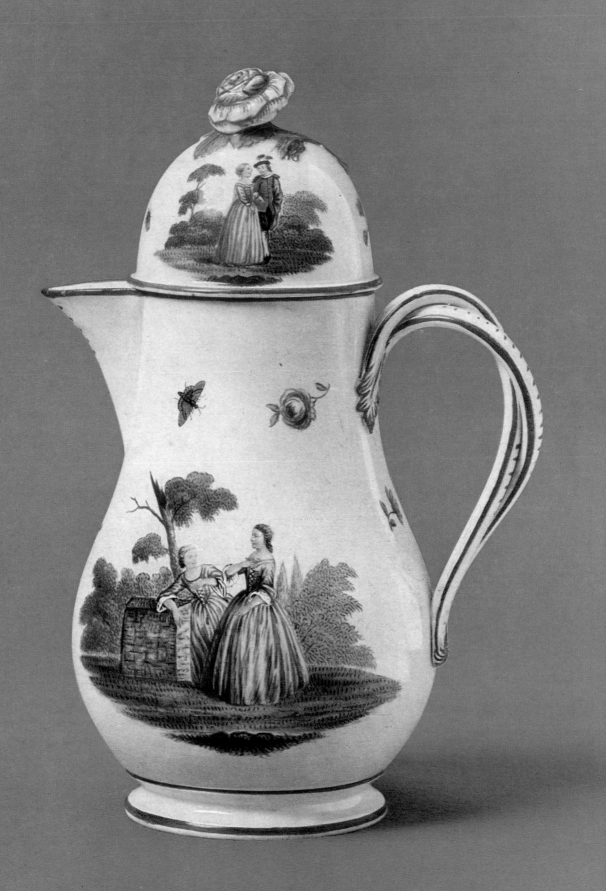

Exhibitions were held throughout Great Britain, and the Ceramic Society sponsored a special series of meetings as a memorial to Josiah.

In the autumn of the bicentenary year, Frank Wedgwood, the much-loved head of the firm, died suddenly. He had joined the works in 1889. He was also High Sheriff of Staffordshire and a Deputy Lieutenant of the county.

Meanwhile four members of the sixth generation joined the firm. Josiah, a 28-year-old economist, whose father, Member of Parliament for Newcastle-under-Lyme, subsequently became first Baron Wedgwood of Barlaston, joined in 1928. He succeeded Frank as managing director in 1930 and became the firm's chairman in 1947. Hensleigh Cecil joined at the age of 20, in 1927; he was destined to spend most of his time in America. Clement Tom joined in 1930 at the age of 23. He was director in charge of building and plant until 1950. John Hamilton joined in 1931 aged 23. In 1927 Norman Wilson joined the company as works manager at the age of 25. Being a highly skilled ceramist, he was able to introduce new and unusual glazes, and continued his experimental work with glazes and new coloured clay bodies.

The bicentenary came at the beginning of the great slump of the thirties and it was indeed fortunate that the firm had a team of young, resourceful and energetic men to cope with it. Between them the four young Wedgwoods, together with Norman Wilson, tackled the problems of the time with urgency and with new ideas. Their most far-reaching decision will be dealt with in the next chapter, but their innovations in the field of design may be mentioned here.

A series of designers from outside the firm were commissioned to enlarge the scope of the Wedgwood range. Among them were such eminent designers and artists as Arnold Machin, Eric Ravilious and Keith Murray. The sculptor John Skeaping had already been commissioned by Frank Wedgwood in 1926. Ravilious had a particular talent for interpreting in modern terms the sober elegance of early Wedgwood creamware; his version of the Regency 'Agricultural Implements' was particularly successful. His death on active service in the war was a great loss to the world of art in general and to ceramic design in

11. Queen's Ware coffee pot with hand enamelling c. 1780. The shape of the pot is number 1422 in the oldest surviving shape book of 1802.

D

particular. Another successful designer of these years was Keith Murray. As an architect — he later designed the new Wedgwood factory — he was fascinated by the clear functional shapes and sharp precise decoration made possible by lathe turning, and he used this traditional process in a contemporary manner.

In 1935, on the retirement of John Goodwin, Victor Skellern became art director, and was able to co-ordinate all this activity. He began his career in the factory, then studied at the Royal College of Art, where he became an Associate of the College before returning to Wedgwood, bringing with him not only the creative abilities of an artist but a wide background of technical knowledge and craftsmanship. He was head of the Wedgwood design studios for nearly 30 years, during which time his technical knowledge and creative ability did much to bring Wedgwood to the forefront of ceramic design. His untimely death in 1965 was a sad loss to the company, and to the industry.

The Move to Barlaston

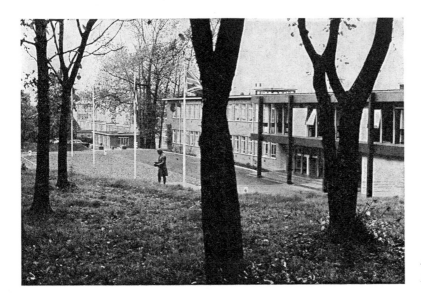

A view of part of the Barlaston factory

I N 1936 the directors came to a decision more important than any other made since the founding of Etruria.

The factory built by Josiah Wedgwood, FRS, was the most up-to-date in the world during his lifetime. By 1936, although it had been radically modernized, it had outlived its usefulness. The eighteenth century workshops, courtyards and the old mill with square open shafting were interesting historically, but not suitable for efficient manufacture.

Furthermore considerable subsidence had taken place in the area as a result of coal-mining beneath it. The factory, instead of being level with the canal, as in the illustration on page 39, was now eight feet below it. This had caused difficulties at the beginning of the twentieth century and there was a threat that the danger might recur. Moreover much of the large estate with which Josiah I had surrounded his factory had been sold in the lean years of the nineteenth century, and dust and dirt from the neighbouring plants presented a further problem: cleanliness is an essential in the making of good pots.

It was therefore decided with great regret to abandon Etruria for a new site six miles away. The example set by Josiah I was followed by his descendants. In 1937 a country estate near the village of Barlaston was bought. The village already had associations with the Wedgwood family, and in nearby Tittensor had lived Sarah, widow of the first Josiah Wedgwood.

Barlaston Park is in pleasant wooded country with open meadows and streams, away from the smoke and grime of the city. There, the new factory was constructed. Nearby a small village of 200 houses has been built. Keith Murray, who has already been mentioned as one of Wedgwood's most successful designers, and his partner, C. S. White were appointed architects for the factory. Louis de Soissons, the architect of Welwyn Garden City, undertook the planning of the village.

The foundation stone was laid in 1938. It was an unusual ceremony. Eight Black Basalt vases had been specially designed by Victor Skellern and produced for the occasion. Queen's Ware cameos bearing the facsimile signatures of the directors were then placed one into each vase. A cameo was added with the name of the late Frank Wedgwood by his son, Tom. Norman Wilson then placed a cameo in the eighth vase on behalf of the management. Eight veteran craftsmen from Etruria, each with over fifty years' service, then placed the vases in a casket and Josiah Wedgwood added a bone china plaque inscribed:

> 'Within this cavity are buried eight pots to commemorate the founding of this factory in a Garden Village in the sixth generation of the descendants of Josiah Wedgwood, who founded his factory at Etruria, Staffordshire, 170 years ago.
>
> "By their works ye shall know them"
>
> September 10. 1938'

The casket was sealed by Alan Wedgwood (assisted by his father, Tom) representing the youngest generation of the family.

The casket was then buried in a vault beneath the entrance of the office block to the strains of Blake's 'Jerusalem', a hymn which recalled a great artist who had worked for Wedgwood.

All the mechanical processes and the firing are done by electricity. Most of this is drawn from the national grid, but there is also a power house where steam is generated to drive supplementary turbine generators and is afterwards condensed and used for space heating. It is, of course, important for any pottery to be kept at an even and fairly high temperature.

Firing is by six electric tunnel ovens and Wedgwood was the first firm to bring them into use in this country. Whereas in the old days the ware had to be carefully stacked in the bottle kilns on saggers, fires had to be lit, then allowed to go out so that the kiln could be emptied, all that is now necessary is for the ware to be stacked on a fire-proof trolley which is automatically pulled through an electrically heated tunnel about 100 yards long. This takes several hours in the case of biscuit firing, and when the kiln trucks emerge at the other end, the ware is cool enough to touch and work can start on it immediately. At this stage it is now hard and durable, and from its texture is known as biscuit ware. It can never again be turned back into clay, so that from now on any spoiled work is a complete loss. The thermal efficiency of these tunnel ovens is much greater and the rate of loss, in damaged ware, much less than with any other type of kiln.

The workshops are well lighted and every modern convenience has been provided for the health and comfort of the operatives. There is a large canteen which serves also as a dance hall, theatre and cinema, according to the many demands made upon it. There are seventeen acres of sports ground for football, cricket, tennis, a bowling green and a handsome pavilion which was provided by the directors in 1959 as a bicentenary gift to the employees. Nearby are two large lakes, well stocked with fish by the angling society; and other amenities cater for a wide variety of recreational activities, under the aegis of the Sports and Social Club. These are financed by employees' contributions which are usually matched by an equal amount from the directors.

Wedgwood was one of the first firms to introduce the Whitley Council machinery of joint consultation between workers and management. The Works Committee (founded in 1920), whose members are elected from the various departments, is an extremely valuable body. It deals with social and welfare problems, but also frequently has sound advice to offer the Board on problems directly affecting production.

Production started at Barlaston in 1940 although the factory was not yet complete. But the war had begun, and with it the immediate dislocation of the pottery trade. By a voluntary concentration scheme operated by the potters themselves, many of the smaller factories without a large export trade were closed, but Wedgwood, with its highly developed market in the U.S., was particularly well placed to be of service in the hard currency export drive of the first years of the war, and continued in operation. Over eighty per cent of its output was exported. Owing to increased productivity the factory was able to maintain its sales, though the number of workers was very considerably reduced and many of the executives joined the armed forces. Much of the factory went over to the production of 'utility' white ware for the home market.

Immediately after the war, building began again. The Queen's Ware section of the factory was considerably extended, and a new china section built by 1949, thus enabling the production of Queen's Ware, bone china and Jasper to be carried out in the new factory. At about the same time, having seen his life's work crowned with success, Clement Tom Wedgwood took the courageous decision of uprooting himself and moving to Rhodesia. Several years before he had undergone a serious operation and, although his recovery had been remarkable, a complete change was now a medical necessity. He died, aged only 52, in 1960.

On Tom's retirement, Norman Wilson, who joined the board in 1946, took complete charge of production.

Etruria continued in use until June 13th, 1950, the date on which in 1769 Josiah I had thrown his 'First Day's' vases. On this day, exactly 181 years later, six 'Last Day's' vases, replicas of the early pieces, were thrown, and Etruria, the factory from which a whole town had grown, ceased production as a pottery.

In 1947 the chairman, Kennard Lawrence Wedgwood, retired after more than fifty years' service, forty-one of which he had spent in the U.S.A. He died in 1950.

Kennard was succeeded as chairman by Josiah. He had pioneered the development of the new factory and now set about steering the company through the problems of post-war expansion.

In New York the duties of president of the American company were taken over by Hensleigh Wedgwood and under his supervision elegant new showrooms were constructed in 1948 at 24 East 54th Street and in the same year the Canadian Company was incorporated in Toronto. Hensleigh retired in 1960 and was succeeded as president by Arthur Bryan, previously general sales manager in England.

In 1955 an Australian Company was formed under the direction of Ian Taylor.

In London the showroom had been closed since 1940, but during the war, with considerable foresight Josiah Wedgwood had acquired valuable premises in the West End. They survived the bombing and in 1948 showrooms and extensive offices were opened at 34 Wigmore Street.

An important part of Wedgwood sales in the United Kingdom are handled through the 'Wedgwood Rooms' — specialist shops within large stores, of which there are over seventy in various parts of the country. The staff are Wedgwood trained and the stocks controlled by Wedgwood, although the Rooms themselves operate as an integral part of the stores in which they are situated. The development of the Wedgwood Rooms was something entirely new in the field of fine china marketing. Yet, as early as 1767, Josiah I had seen the need for something of this kind and wrote to Bentley 'to explain to you my reasons for wanting a *Large* Room. It was not to shew, or have a large stock of ware in Town, but to enable me to shew various Table and desert [sic] services completely set out on two ranges of Tables, six or eight at least such services are absolutely necessary to be shewn in order to *do the needful* with the Ladys in the neatest, genteelest and best method. And beside room *for my Ware*, I must have more room *for my Ladys* for they sometimes come in very large shoals together.' The Wedgwood Rooms of today, with their spacious planning and specially designed equipment, translate this idea into modern terms.

At the end of 1960, the Hon. Josiah Wedgwood, who had led the firm as Managing Director for 32 years, and had probably contributed more than anyone since his great-great-great-grandfather, decided to retire from this position, and remain as Chairman. His cousin, Sir John Wedgwood, who had worked with him since 1931, was Deputy Chairman until his retirement in 1966. The Hon. Josiah was succeeded by Norman Wilson and F. Maitland Wright (whose wife was a daughter of Frank Wedgwood) as joint Managing

Directors. They retired in 1963. Two Wedgwood descendants, Dr. John Wedgwood and Dr. Alan F. Wedgwood subsequently joined the Board.

The Fifties were a period of great expansion, following the restrictions of the war and post-war austerity. As in the Thirties, there came a flood of new designs, though demand for Jasper continued to increase, and by the end of the decade its production, in value, was twenty-seven times the pre-war figure. Lithography was greatly developed as a technique for decoration, for which its flexibility made it specially appropriate, and a number of new shapes were designed. Norman Wilson perfected a technique of making tableware from two-coloured clays which greatly stimulated demand for Queen's Ware. The Barlaston factory, fortunately set in a spacious estate, spilled out beyond its original area, and by the end of the Fifties employed over 2,000 people.

On May 1st 1959, the company commemorated the bicentenary of the foundation of the firm. Celebrations throughout the year included a comprehensive exhibition of Wedgwood at the Victoria and Albert Museum and another at the Royal Scottish Museum in Edinburgh. A travelling exhibition also toured the large towns, and there were special displays in shops throughout the world. Articles were written in collectors' and connoisseurs' journals everywhere, and thirty American members of the fourth Wedgwood International Seminar 1959 came to England for a week to study the Wedgwood collections in this country. In 1969, for the bicentenary of the opening of the Etruria factory, the Wedgwood International Seminar came to England again for their fourteenth meeting, and such had been the growth of interest in Wedgwood collecting in the intervening decade, that the party now consisted of 180 members who travelled the country for three weeks, and sat for three days

12. A bone china plate is skilfully enamelled. The pattern is Turquoise Florentine.

OVERLEAF

13. Quince and Blue Pacific oven-to-tableware. Modern productions to meet the requirements of informal living.

14. Two designs which were first produced a century ago and still in current production — Columbia 595 and Turquoise Florentine.

15. Oven-to-tableware, Iona Pattern.

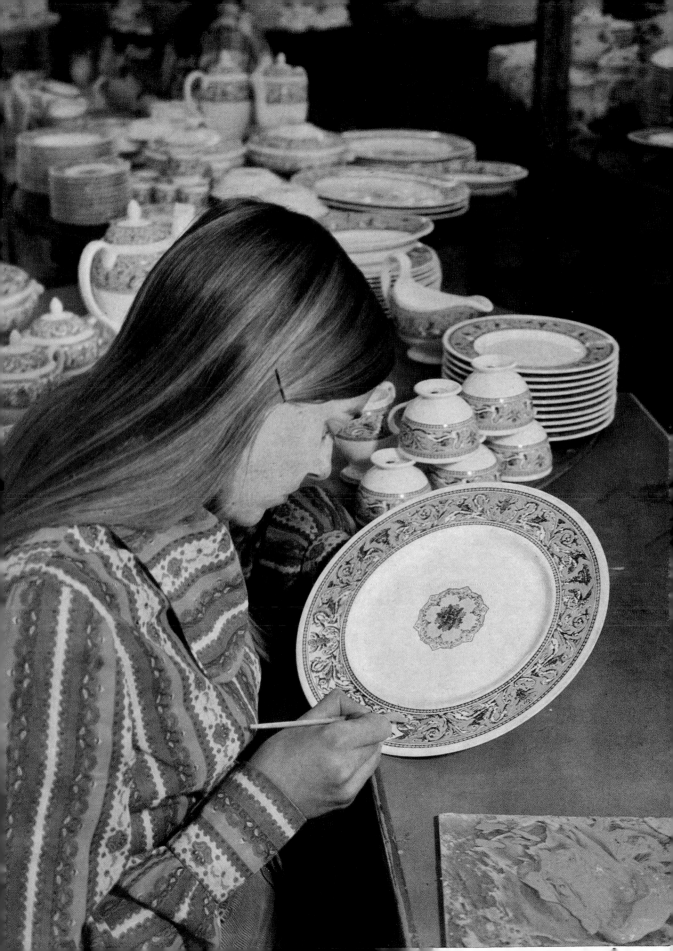

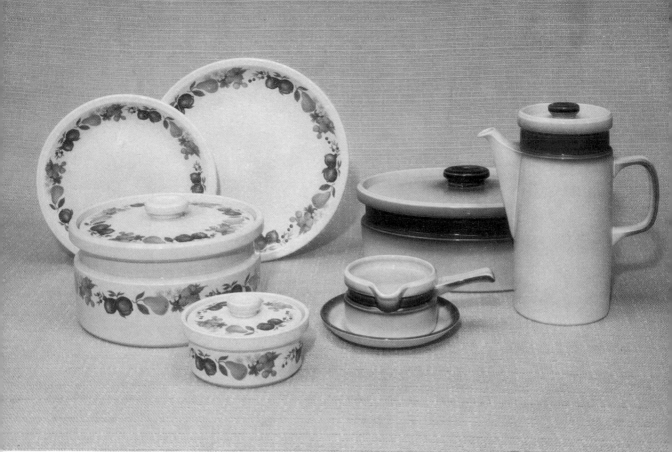

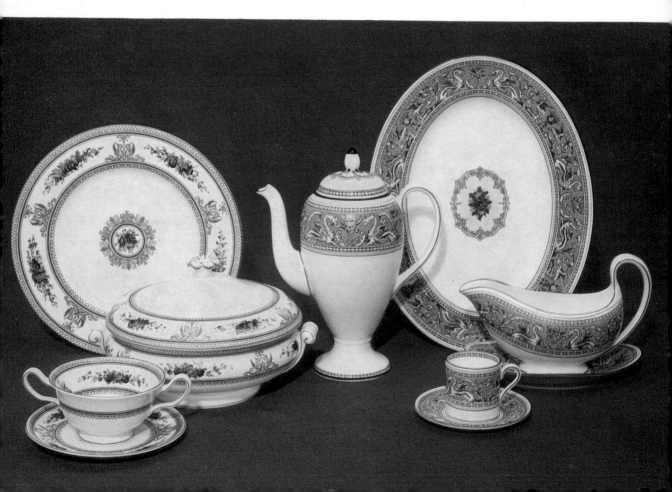

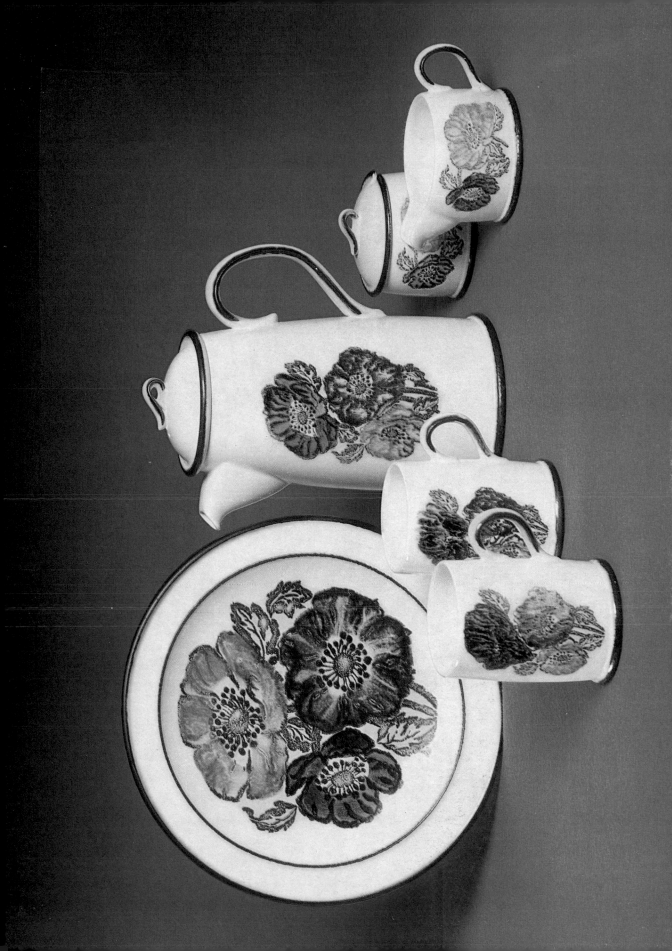

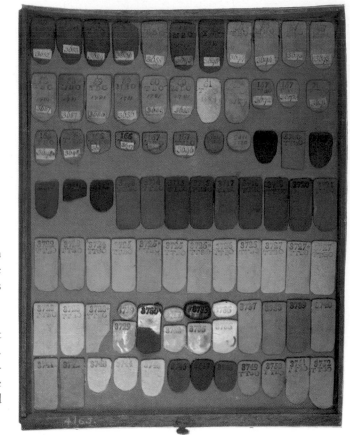

16. One of about 3,000 trials which Wedgwood conducted in the 1770's in order to perfect his Jasper Ware.

17. The Wedgwood factory at Barlaston, near Stoke-on-Trent. This factory first went into production in 1940 superseding the factory at Etruria which had been in operation since 1769.

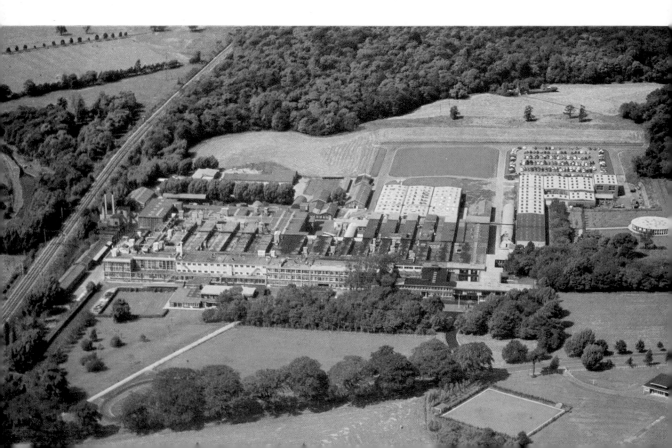

in the Victoria and Albert lecture theatre, listening to specialist lectures on Wedgwood ware of all periods. The English Wedgwood Society and the American Societies in many cities do much to further historical study of the ware, and its collection. Until the 1960's the Wedgwood firm, though growing larger and larger, still remained substantially in its original form. In an age, however, of take-over and amalgamation, when larger units became essential for efficient and economical production, Wedgwood expanded dramatically, by taking over, within a few years, a whole series of other pottery businesses, each making a special contribution to the group.

The first firm to be taken over, in January 1966, was that of William Adams and Sons, a firm which traced its history back over three centuries. In about 1640, one of the Adams family built himself a house which, because of its unusual building material, in an area of stone or wooden houses, came to be known as the Brick House; in 1657, the most important pottery works in the area was built beside it. As we have seen earlier, Josiah Wedgwood leased this Brick House Works early in his career, and produced his ware there for 11 years, maintaining his lease there for several years after the Etruria factory was opened. At the end of the seventeenth century, Adams is credited with the introduction of salt-glazed ware into Staffordshire, where it remained the staple manufacture until the time when Josiah Wedgwood was a young man. At the time of the take-over by Wedgwood, the main product of the factory was earthenware, including a very attractive variety called 'Calyx', with a characteristic pale green glaze, and hand-painted decoration in various patterns, mostly derived from eighteenth century originals.

There were two other acquisitions the same year — Royal Tuscan and Susie Cooper. Founded in 1881, Royal Tuscan now manufacture bone china specially designed and produced for the hotel and catering industry, while Susie Cooper, founded in 1937, is one of the most distinctive names in the bone china trade. The only woman Royal Designer for Industry in the ceramic tableware manufacturing industry, Miss Cooper has designed every pattern in the company's range. She has since designed a number of patterns for Wedgood bone china, which are produced over the 'Wedgwood–Susie Cooper' backstamp.

In 1967, the firm of Coalport became part of the Wedgwood Group. Established in Shropshire in the 18th century, and said to have been the source of that most famous of Chinoiserie designs, the Willow Pattern, the company moved to the Potteries in the 1920's. It now produces a wide variety of tableware and ornamental pieces, including the Coalbrookdale collectors' items. Floral china is a speciality.

The year 1968 was a memorable one in the story of Wedgwood when its size was doubled with the acquisition of the large-scale earthenware manu-facturing business of Johnson Brothers. Founded in 1883, the firm eventually grew into an 'empire' of five tableware factories, one sanitaryware factory and manufacturing companies overseas.

In 1969 the group made its entry into the glass industry through the acquisition of King's Lynn Glass, Norfolk (now Wedgwood Glass) manu-facturing modern glassware near the Norfolk coast. This company was established in 1966 and the factory is the most up-to-date of its type in Britain; in 1972, the King's Lynn factory was considerably extended and its output of glassware and hand cut lead crystal was doubled. In the same year, Merseyside Jewellers of Liverpool was acquired. This company had, for some years, mounted Jasper cameos for the production of Wedgwood jewellery; an operation which was entirely transferred to the Barlaston factory in 1970.

At the beginning of the 1970's there was yet another major move. The acquisition of the J & G Meakin and Midwinter companies made the Wedgwood Group one of the largest fine china and earthenware manufacturers in the world. Midwinter has an international reputation for producing outstanding modern designs in fine earthenware. Founded in 1910 by William Midwinter, father of the present designer and director, W. Roy Midwinter, the company merged, in 1968, with J & G Meakin, a famous name in the earthenware tableware industry since 1851.

In 1973 a further three companies were acquired by the Wedgwood Group. Crown Staffordshire, founded in 1810, was a family-controlled firm until 1964; the company was among the pioneers in the introduction of bone china flowers for ornamental use. Mason's Ironstone was founded in 1795 and the famous Ironstone patent was taken out in 1813, and the original patterns and shapes continue to be produced to the present day. Precision Studios, manufacturers of decorative materials for the ceramic tableware industry, was founded in 1958; the main production is in the field of highly specialized silk-screen ceramic transfers.

At the end of 1971 the group acquired the important London specialist fine china retail business of Gered, with two leading retail outlets in the West End of London and formerly a major customer of Wedgwood for many years. To complete a busy eight years of growth, there came the acquisition in 1974 of a second glass company, Galway Crystal Limited. Founded in Galway, Ireland, in 1967 the company has established a high reputation for its exquisitely cut crystal.

Meanwhile, the Wedgwood factory itself has been expanding rapidly. The original Barlaston layout was designed for about 1,000 workers, and had long since proved inadequate for the growing numbers who worked there. Numerous extensions have been made over the years, culminating in a £1,000,000 scheme recently completed. Among the new sections is a delightful circular design studio, which gives the designers, for the first time, accommodation appropriate to their importance in the firm's achievements. It was opened by Lord Snowdon.

In 1966, Wedgwood was among the first to receive the Queen's Award to Industry. This is given for outstanding contributions to export, and over 60 per cent of the wares made in the group's factories are sold abroad. A further Queen's Award was given in 1971.

In May 1967, Wedgwood shares were introduced on the Stock Exchange, a move exemplifying the firm's growth and diversification. Up to that time it had been a private company, which until the end of 1967 had had, as successive Chairmen, only descendants of the original Josiah Wedgwood. The fifth Josiah retired at the end of that year, and became Honorary Life President; he died a few months later.

His successor was Arthur Bryan who had first joined the firm as a management trainee in 1947. A young protégé of the Hon. Josiah Wedgwood — who characteristically foresaw him as a likely chief executive — Arthur Bryan was

trained in all departments of the Company, and held posts as London
Manager, General Sales Manager and President of the American Company.
His outstanding success as a senior executive confirmed the earlier expectations
of Josiah Wedgwood and F. Maitland Wright. Anxious to safeguard the
traditions and future progress of the Company, the directors recalled him to
England in 1963 as Managing Director of Wedgwood — the first man outside
the family to head the firm. In 1968 he became Chairman and in the same year
was appointed Her Majesty's Lieutenant for the County of Staffordshire, one
of the few industrialists and among the youngest men to hold the post.
Peter Williams who had joined Wedgwood in 1956 as Company Secretary
was appointed to the Board in 1962. He became Finance Director of the
parent company in 1966. In 1968 he was appointed Joint Managing Director
with Arthur Bryan who at that time took up his new appointment as Chairman.
Peter Williams became Deputy Chairman in March 1975.

Today, Wedgwood and its group of companies — with nearly 9,000
employees in 20 factories — account for about one-fifth of the British
ceramic tableware industry's output and for about a quarter of its exports.
This is an extraordinary change since the days of Etruria; the first Josiah,
however, would look with admiration at the way in which, in its third
century, the Group which bears his name is responding to the opportunities
and challenges of the times.

Wedgwood Trade Marks

The backstamps below are in current use, and purchasers should look carefully for them. If none of them appears on a piece it is probably not Wedgwood.

The single word WEDGWOOD is impressed or printed on some Queen's Ware (fine earthenware) and on all Jasper and Black Basalt. Since 1891 the words 'Made in England' have been added to comply with U.S. tariff regulations. The name of the pattern is also sometimes added and the names Etruria and Barlaston.

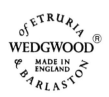

A mark similar to the one on the right is now printed on most Wedgwood Queen's Ware (fine earthenware) and sometimes the pattern name is included with it.

The mark showing a replica of the Portland Vase and bearing the word 'WEDGWOOD' was introduced in 1878 and has been used on Wedgwood bone china ever since. 'MADE IN ENGLAND' was added in 1891, and 'BONE CHINA' in 1937.

The word WEDGWOOD and the replica of the Portland Vase are registered Trade Marks of Josiah Wedgwood & Sons Ltd., whose business was founded by Josiah Wedgwood, FRS, in 1759. Since then other pottery concerns whose name includes the word Wedgwood have come into existence, but they have no connection whatever with Josiah Wedgwood & Sons Ltd. and their products are *not* WEDGWOOD WARE.

wedgwood

Probably the first mark. Supposed to have been used by Josiah Wedgwood at Burslem 1759–69.

WEDGWOOD

This is a very rare mark, used at the Bell Works 1764–9.

WEDGWOOD

WEDGWOOD

Used in varying sizes from 1759–69.

The circular stamp, without the inner and outer rings, and without the word Etruria is doubtless the earliest form of the Wedgwood and Bentley stamp, 1769.

This mark, with the word Etruria, was fixed in the corner, inside the plinth of old basalt vases. It is sometimes found on the pedestal of a bust or large figure, 1769–80.

This circular stamp, with an inner and outer line, was always placed around the screw of the basalt, granite and Etruscan vases, but is never found on Jasper vases, 1769–80.

Unique script mark. Wedgwood & Bentley, 1769–80.

Wedgwood
& Bentley
356

Mark used on Wedgwood & Bentley intaglios, with the catalogue number varying in size, 1769–80.

W. & B.

Very small intaglios were sometimes marked W&B with the catalogue number, or simply with the number only, 1769–80.

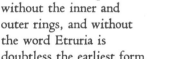

Rare mark found only on chocolate and white seal intaglios, usually portraits made of two layers of clay with the edges polished for mounting, 1769–80.

WEDGWOOD
& BENTLEY

Wedgwood
& Bentley

These marks, varying in size are found upon busts, granite and basalt vases, figures, plaques, medallions and cameos, from the largest tablet to the smallest cameo, 1769–80.

WEDGWOOD

Wedgwood

WEDGWOOD

WEDGWOOD

Varying in size, these marks are attributed to the period after Bentley's death (1780) and probably used for a time after Josiah's death (1795).

WEDGWOOD & SONS

Very rare mark used for a short period in 1790.

JOSIAH WEDGWOOD Feb. 2nd 1805

Mark of Josiah Wedgwood II. Supposedly a new partnership or change in the firm. Found only on some basalt tripod incense burners. It may be the date when the design was first registered, 1805. Sometimes '2nd Feby' appears instead of 'Feb. 2'.

WEDGWOOD

The mark upon the bone china or porcelain, made 1812–28, always printed either in red, blue or in gold.

WEDGWOOD
Wedgwood

From 1769 to the present day this mark has been impressed in the clay on Queen's Ware, or printed in colour. In recent times the words Etruria and Barlaston and the name of the pattern have in many cases been printed in addition to the trade mark. From 1780, ornamental Jasper, Black Basalt, cane, terra cotta and Queen's Ware are always marked with this stamp. The name 'England' was added in 1891.

WEDGWOOD
ETRURIA
WEDGWOOD
ETRURIA
Wedgwood
Etruria

These marks are rarely found on pieces of a very high character. Adopted about 1840 but used for only a short period.

WEDGWOOD

This mark, for bone china, was adopted in 1878 when the manufacture of bone china was revived.

ENGLAND

England was added to the mark Wedgwood in 1891 to comply with the American Customs Regulation known as the McKinley Tariff Act.

WEDGWOOD®
Bone China
MADE IN ENGLAND

Mark used today on bone china, developed from mark of 1878.

of ETRURIA
WEDGWOOD®
& MADE IN
ENGLAND
BARLASTON

This mark is used today on Queen's Ware, starting in 1940.

Glossary of Terms Used in the Text

Agate Pottery made to resemble agate stone by kneading together clays of contrasting colours, so that the streaky pattern extends through the body.

Ball Clay A clay mined in Dorset and Devon. An important ingredient of earthenware and stoneware. It gives plasticity and strength to the pottery body.

Biscuit Ware which has been fired once but not glazed.

Black Basalt A fine grained black stoneware made by staining the body with manganese dioxide and cobalt. Perfected by Wedgwood in 1768.

Body The name given to the composite materials in plastic form as used by the potters, e.g. earthenware or china body.

Bone China A hard vitreous body about half of which is calcined animal bone, the remainder being mainly china stone and china clay. It is noted for its great strength, whiteness and translucency.

Cameo Ornament in relief, usually one colour on a background of another colour. Originally these were of semi-precious stones; Wedgwood used the name for his smaller Jasper pieces.

Caneware Pale buff-coloured stoneware made from 1770.

Carrara An unglazed smooth porcelain in imitation of Parian or Carrara marble much used in Victorian times by many potters under the name of Parian ware. Used at Etruria about 1860.

Celadon Originally a pale green porcelain glaze used by the Chinese. Wedgwood used the name to describe a self-coloured green earthenware.

China Clay (Kaolin) The whitest clay known. It is found in Cornwall, England, and is derived from granite rock which has undergone decomposition over a long period of time.

China Stone Known also as Cornish stone. At high temperatures it becomes a hard white glass-like substance.

Cream-Coloured Ware A light-coloured English earthenware first made about 1750 which varied considerably in character, quality and colour. It was on the manufacture of 'Cream Colour' that Josiah Wedgwood, FRS, built up his business.
See *Queen's Ware*.

Dry Bodies Non-porous unglazed stoneware bodies originally made from local marls sometimes stained with colouring oxides. Basalt, caneware, Jasper and rosso antico are dry bodies.

Earthenware All opaque ware which is

E

porous after the first or 'biscuit' firing. The chief ingredients are flint, ball clay, china stone and china clay. Wedgwood early perfected the technique of staining this white 'body' with durable colours as in their Celadon, Lavender, Windsor Grey, Havana, Cane, etc. If chipped the same colour is revealed throughout the ware.

Engine-Turning Lathe   A lathe equipped with an eccentric motion, built for Josiah Wedgwood about 1763 by Matthew Boulton and used to incise decorations on ware before firing. One of the original lathes is still in use at Barlaston.

Etruscan Ware   Black Basalt, with encaustic decoration mainly in red or white in imitation of early Etruscan ware.

Firing   *Enamel Decorations:* All kilns at Wedgwood are electrically fired. Some 40 years ago kilns were usually muffled coal-firing devices for firing on-glaze decorations or hardening on underglaze colours, prior to glazing, at temperatures ranging from 750° to 900°C. These firing processes are now carried out in electric tunnel kilns.

    Biscuit and Glost: With the advent of the tunnel kiln, the term 'oven' has fallen into disuse. Electrically fired biscuit tunnel kilns fire clayware up to 1200°C. for earthenware, and 1300°C.

for bone china. Glost tunnel kilns fire the glaze at temperatures around 1100°C.

    Ovens: Bottle-necked, coal-firing devices, which are gradually becoming obsolete. There are none at Wedgwood.

Glaze   A glassy preparation applied in liquid form to the surface of biscuit ware and then fired, which enhances its appearance and makes it impervious to liquids. It is usually brilliant though in 1933 Wedgwood introduced many matt glazes, including matt white 'Moonstone' and, in 1958, matt black 'Ravenstone'.

Intaglio   A sunken or incised design, the opposite of a cameo. In the eighteenth century many were made for seals, rings, etc.

Jasper   A hard vitreous body, which can be stained by the addition of metallic oxides to a variety of colours. Invented by Josiah Wedgwood, FRS, in 1774.

Kaolin   See China Clay.

Lustre   An iridescent or metallic film on the surface of ware obtained by the use of metallic oxides, gold, silver, copper, platinum. First used by Wedgwood in 1805 in the purple and gold 'moonlight lustre'.

Porcelain   A vitreous, semi-translucen-body originally made from a mixture of a white clay, felt

	spathic stone and silica, e.g. Chinese, Dresden, Plymouth and Bristol. Soft porcelain contains similar ingredients with the addition of materials to form a glass when fired and to give the 'paste' greater translucency, e.g. Chelsea, Bow, Nantgarw, etc.
Pot Bank	Potworks, factory or place where clay products are manufactured.
Pottery	Most fired clay wares of whatever type or class including sanitary ware, internal tiles, garden ware, kitchen crockery, table and ornamental wares.
Queen's Ware	The name used exclusively for Wedgwood's fine earthenware. Permission for the use of the name was given by Queen Charlotte who was much impressed by Wedgwood's product.
Rosso Antico	Fine red unglazed stoneware made by Wedgwood as a refinement of Elers Ware— see *Dry Bodies*.
Salt Glaze	Stoneware glazed by throwing common salt into the kiln when it reaches its maximum temperature.
Stoneware	A hard vitreous body fired at a high temperature.
Throwing	The process of forming pottery on a potter's wheel. A ball of clay is thrown upon the revolving wheel, centred and worked into shape with the hands.
Tortoiseshell	An effect produced in a lead glaze by dusting metallic oxides, such as manganese, cobalt or copper, over the surface of the ware.
Transfer Printing	A method of decoration in which patterns are transferred to the ware by means of a tissue paper transfer printed with special ceramic colours from an engraved copper plate. Sadler & Green of Liverpool perfected the process in 1756, using copper-plate engravings. In 1763 Josiah I bought the right to do his own printing.
	Nowadays multi-coloured decorations can also be applied to pottery by lithographs and silk-screen transfers.

The various processes used in the manufacture of pottery are fully described and illustrated in the book *The Making of Wedgwood* obtainable from Josiah Wedgwood & Sons Ltd., Barlaston, Stoke-on-Trent.

E2

Books on Wedgwood

BIOGRAPHIES, FAMILY HISTORIES AND PEDIGREES

LLEWELLYN JEWITT, *The Wedgwoods, being a life of Josiah Wedgwood* (Virtue & Co., 1865)

ELIZA METEYARD, *The Life of Josiah Wedgwood*, 2 volumes (Hurst and Blackett, 1865–6)

SAMUEL SMILES, *Josiah Wedgwood* (John Murray, 1894)

SIR ARTHUR H. CHURCH, *Josiah Wedgwood, Master Potter* (Seeley & Co., 1894)

K. E. FARRER (editor), *Wedgwood's Letters*, 3 volumes, 1903–6 (reprint by Fine Masters and Wedgwood)

ELBERT HUBBARD, *Josiah Wedgwood and Sarah* (The Roycrafters, New York, 1906)

JOSIAH C. WEDGWOOD, *A History of the Wedgwood Family* (The St. Catherine Press Ltd., 1908)

JOSIAH C. WEDGWOOD, *Staffordshire Pottery and its History* (Sampson Low, Marston & Co. Ltd.)

JULIA WEDGWOOD, *Personal Life of Josiah Wedgwood* (Macmillan & Co., 1915)

JOSIAH C. WEDGWOOD and JOSHUA G. E. WEDGWOOD, *Wedgwood Pedigrees* (Titus Wilson & Son, 1925)

RALPH M. MOWER, 'The Wedgwoods — Ten Generations of Potters' in *Journal of Economic and Business History*, Vol. IV, No. 2, February, 1932

ROGER FALK, *The Business of Management* (Pelican 1961) — contains a case-history of management in Wedgwood

ANN FINER and GEORGE SAVAGE, *The Selected Letters of Josiah Wedgwood* (Cory, Adams and Mackay, 1965)

WEDGWOOD WARE

ELIZA METEYARD, *Handbook of Wedgwood Ware*, 1875

F. RATHBONE, *Old Wedgwood*, 1893

F. RATHBONE, *Catalogue of the Wedgwood Museum, Etruria*, 1909

G. C. WILLIAMSON, *The Imperial Russian Dinner Service*, 1909

WILLIAM BURTON, *Josiah Wedgwood and his Pottery* (Cassell & Co., 1922)

HARRY BARNARD, *Chats on Wedgwood Ware* (T. Fisher Unwin, 1924)

R. L. HOBSON, *Chinese Porcelain and Wedgwood Pottery* (Lady Lever Art Gallery, 1928)

JEAN GORELY and MARY WADSWORTH, *Old Wedgwood* (Fogg Museum of Art, 1944)

HENSLEIGH C. WEDGWOOD and JOHN MEREDITH GRAHAM, *Wedgwood, a Living Tradition* (The Brooklyn Museum, 1948)

W. B. HONEY, *Wedgwood Ware* (Faber & Faber, 1948)

Early Wedgwood Pottery (Josiah Wedgwood & Sons Ltd., 1951)

WOLF MANKOWITZ, *The Portland Vase and the Wedgwood Copies* (Andre Deutsch, 1952)

WOLF MANKOWITZ, *Wedgwood* (Batsford, 1953)

WOLF MANKOWITZ and REGINALD HAGGAR, *The Concise Encyclopedia of English Pottery and Porcelain* (contains much information on Wedgwood) (Andre Deutsch, 1957)

CAROL MACHT, *Classical Wedgwood Designs* (M. Barrows & Co., 1957)

WEDGWOOD, *Small Picture Book No. 45* (Victoria & Albert Museum, 1958)

Wedgwood Bicentenary Exhibition 1959 (catalogue), Victoria & Albert Museum (issued by Josiah Wedgwood & Sons Ltd.)

HARRY M. BUTEN, *Wedgwood and Artists* (1960) and *Wedgwood Counterpoint* (1962) — the Buten Museum of Wedgwood, Merion, Pa., U.S.A.

Wedgwood ABC 1964

The Making of Wedgwood (Josiah Wedgwood & Sons Ltd. — Revised 1974)

ALISON KELLY, *Decorative Wedgwood in Architecture and Furniture* (Country Life, 1965)

ALISON KELLY, *Wedgwood Ware* (Ward Lock, 1970)

ROBIN REILLY, *Wedgwood Jasper* (Letts, 1972)

GUY MANNERS, *The Wedgwood Portland Vase* (Josiah Wedgwood & Sons Ltd., 1972)

BRUCE TATTERSALL and GUY MANNERS, *Wedgwood at Woburn* (Catalogue, Josiah Wedgwood & Sons Ltd., 1973)

ROBIN REILLY and GEORGE SAVAGE, *Wedgwood; the Portrait Medallions* (Barrie & Jenkins, 1974)

BRUCE TATTERSALL, *Stubbs and Wedgwood* (Tate Gallery, 1974)

WEDGWOOD MUSEUM BARLASTON (Josiah Wedgwood & Sons Ltd. — Revised 1974)

The address of the firm is

JOSIAH WEDGWOOD AND SONS LIMITED
Barlaston, Stoke-on-Trent, Staffs. ST12 9ES

Showrooms and overseas companies:

England	34 Wigmore Street, London, W.1
U.S.A.	555 Madison Avenue, New York 10022
Canada	271 Yorkland Boulevard, Willowdale, Ontario
Australia	234 Clarence Street, Sydney 2000, N.S.W.

Index

Note: Page references to illustrations in colour are in **bold** type

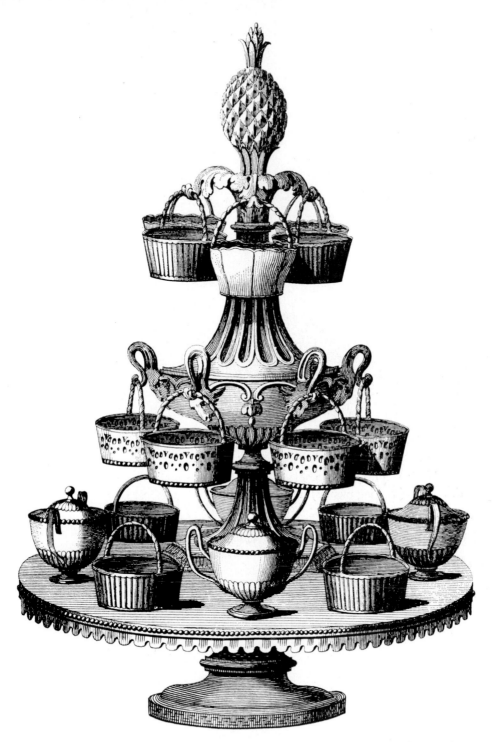

1. Engraving of an epergne, from the Wedgwood 1790–5 catalogue of Queen's Ware shapes. In a style reminiscent of silver shape prototypes. Epergne (French) was the name for a dinner table centrepiece.

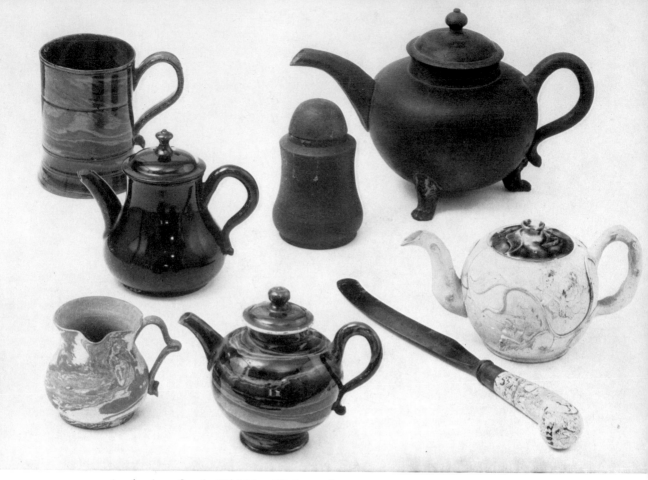

2. A selection of early Whieldon-Wedgwood wares, made in period 1755-8 at Fenton.

3. Saltglaze block moulds c. 1760. Block moulds are the basic moulds from which hollow potter's moulds (working moulds) are made.

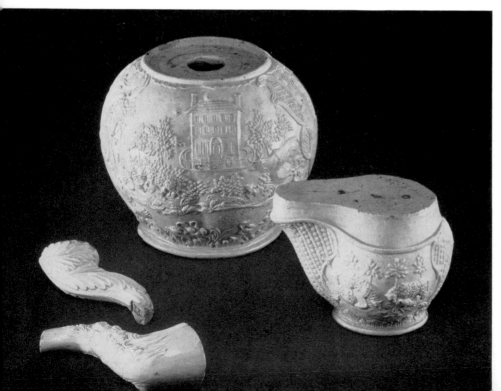

4. TOP RIGHT. Green glaze earthenware teapot, resembling a cauliflower. Wedgwood perfected his green glaze when in partnership with Whieldon.

5. BOTTOM RIGHT. 'Chinoiserie' teapot with variegated body in cream coloured earthenware. Probably modelled by William Greatbatch. Made at Ivy House Works, c. 176- *Castle Museum and Art Gallery Nottingham.*

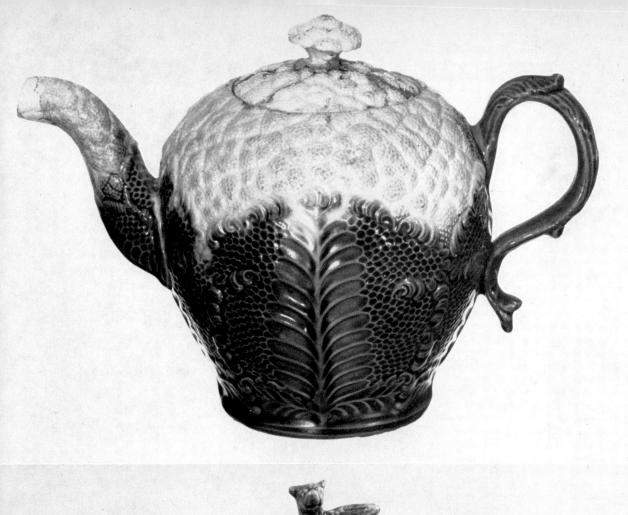

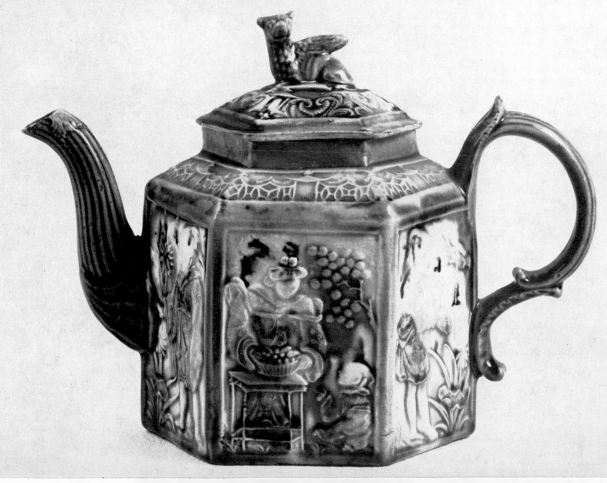

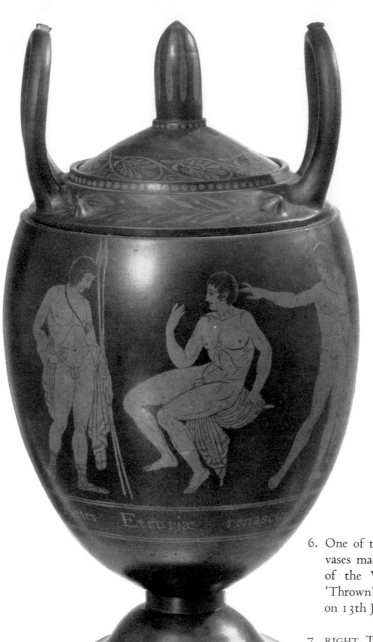

6. One of the six Black Basalt 'First Day's' vases made to commemorate the opening of the Wedgwood factory at Etruria. 'Thrown' at the potter's wheel by Josiah, on 13th June 1769.

7. RIGHT. Two Black Basalt vases, both Shape No. 1 in Wedgwood's 1770 shape book. Marked 'Wedgwood and Bentley', made 1775.

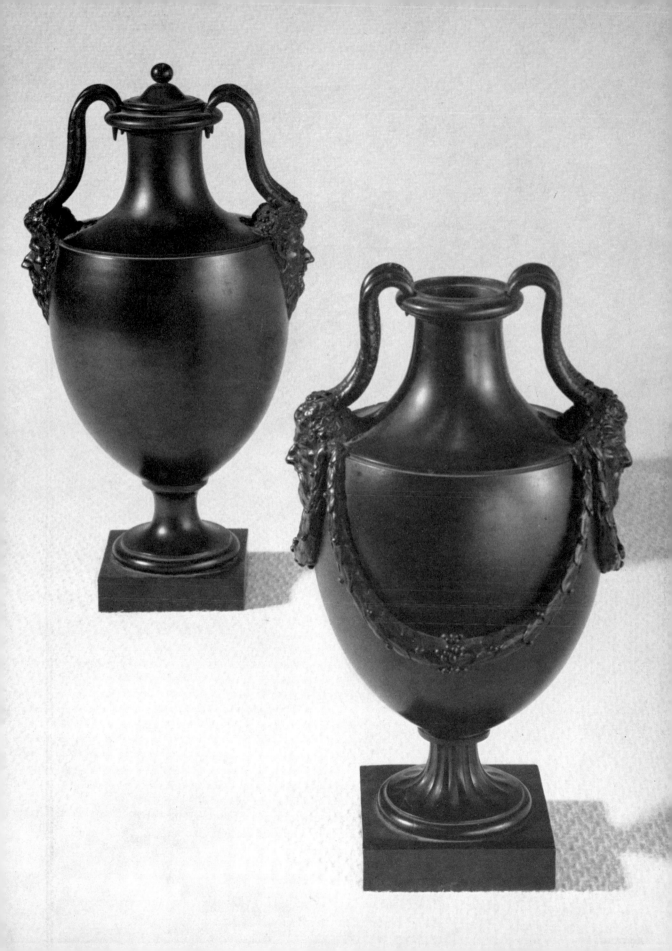

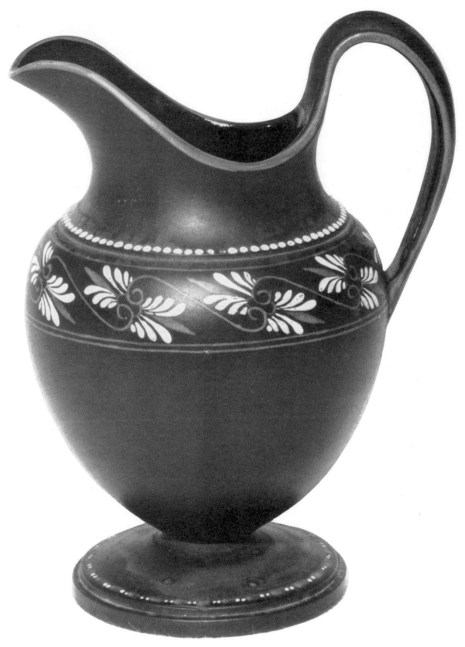

8. Black Basalt cream jug decorated with 'Running Anthemion' design in encaustic colours. Marked 'Wedgwood and Bentley', c. 1770.

9. RIGHT. Wine and water vases in Black Basalt. Left, 'Sacred to Bacchus' wine vase, right, 'Sacred to Neptune' water vase. Both marked 'Wedgwood and Bentley', 16 inches high and made at Etruria in 1775.

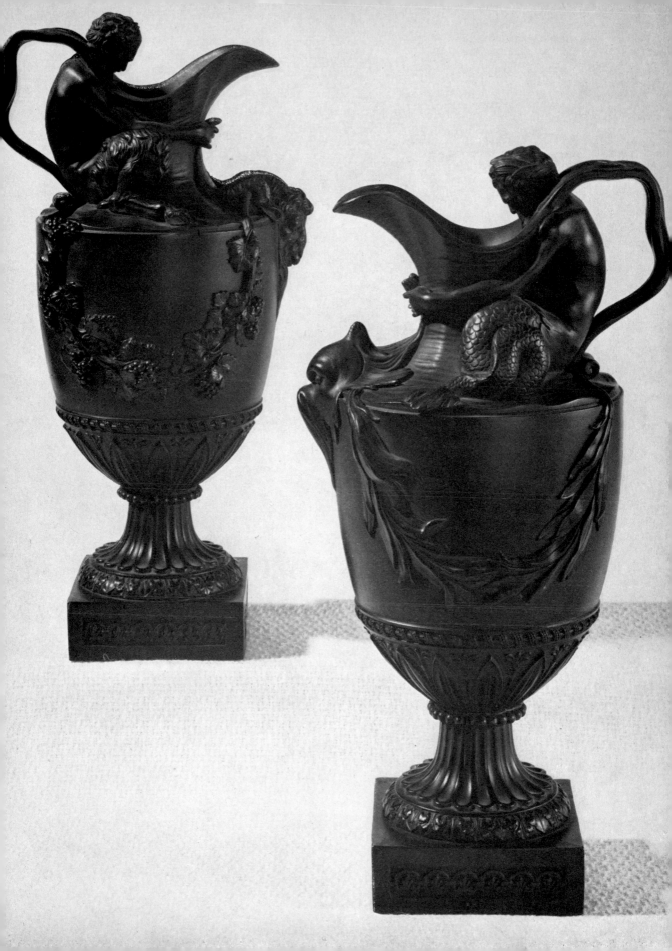

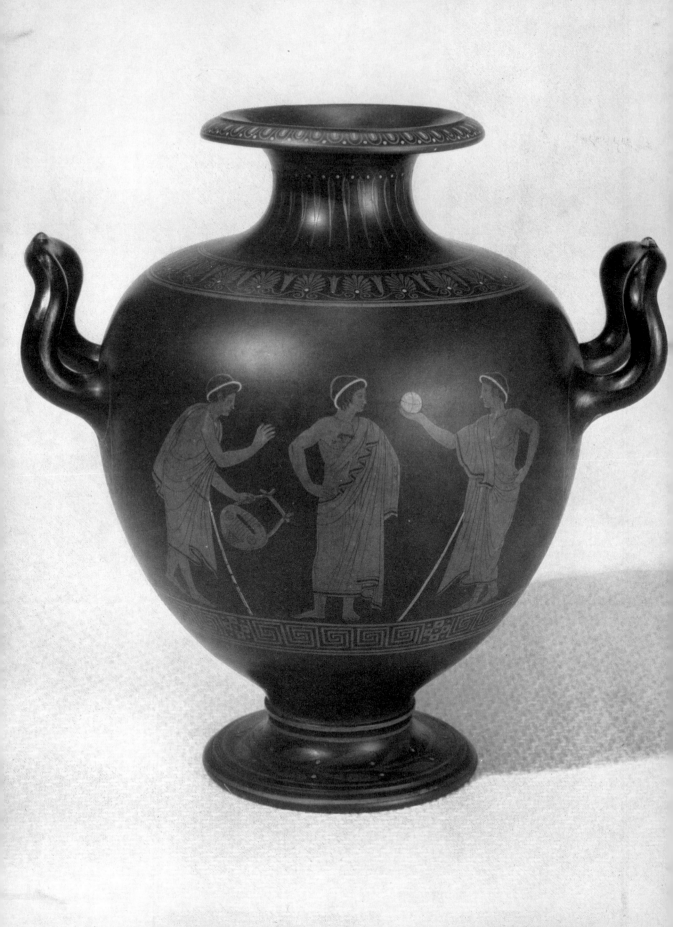

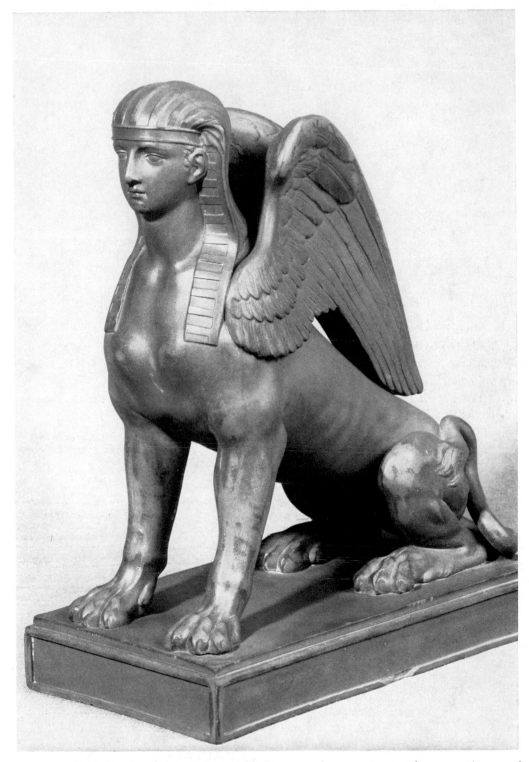

10. LEFT. Black Basalt vase made in Josiah's No. 111 shape, c. 1775. The encaustic enamel decoration is derived from Greek red figure vases.

11. ABOVE. Rosso Antico sphinx candlestick. One of a pair made at Etruria, c. 1780. *City of Liverpool Museums.*

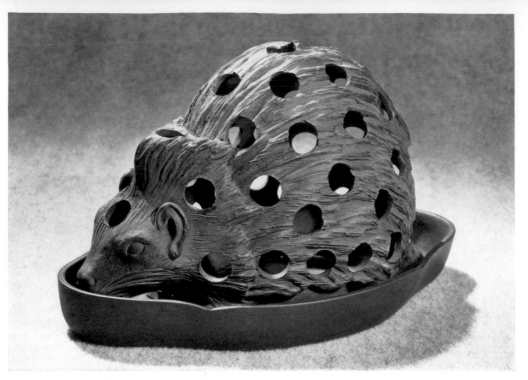

12. Hedgehog bulb pot in Black Basalt, c. 1780. The pot was filled with soil and the bulbs, probably crocus, were pushed into the surface of the soil, so that their spikes grew through the holes.

13. BELOW. Basalt Black bust of Ben Jonson, 1787, and Black Basalt statue entitled 'Mercury on the Rock', 1786. Both marked 'Wedgwood', height 18 inches.

14. RIGHT. Two Queen's Ware vases glazed to resemble the stones, agate and porphyry. Both marked 'Wedgwood and Bentley', c. 1775. The lid of the lefthand vase is reversed, to show use as candleholder.

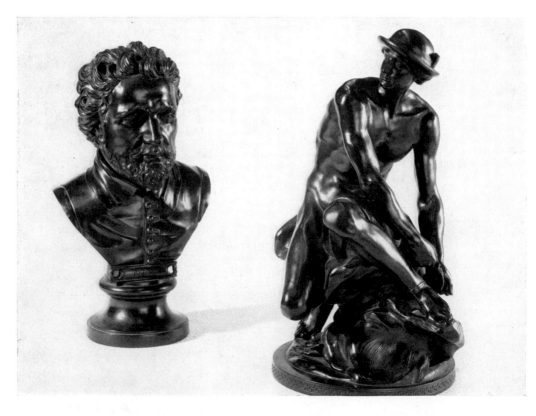

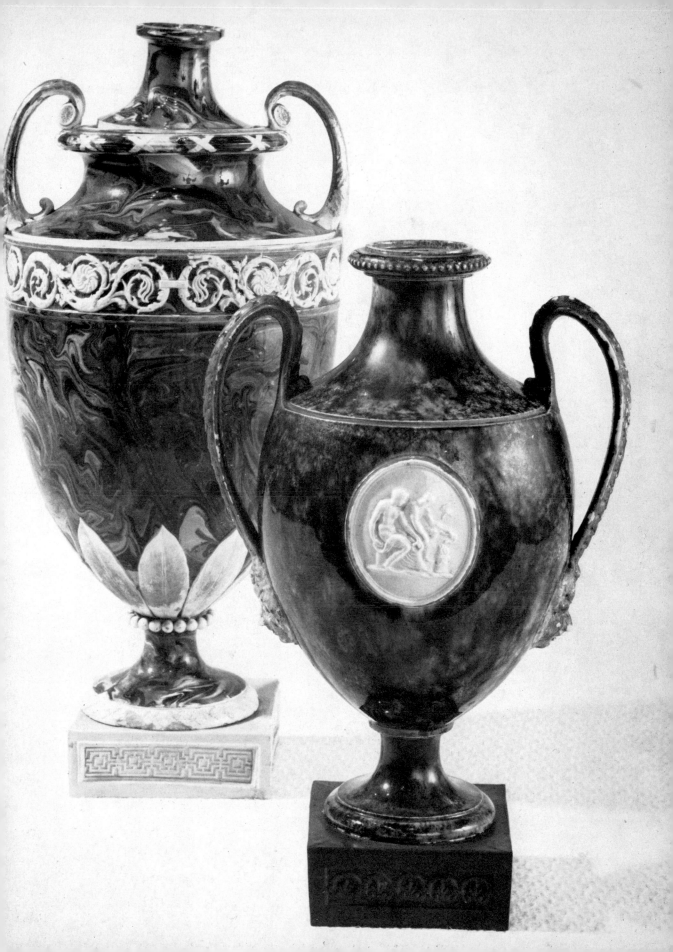

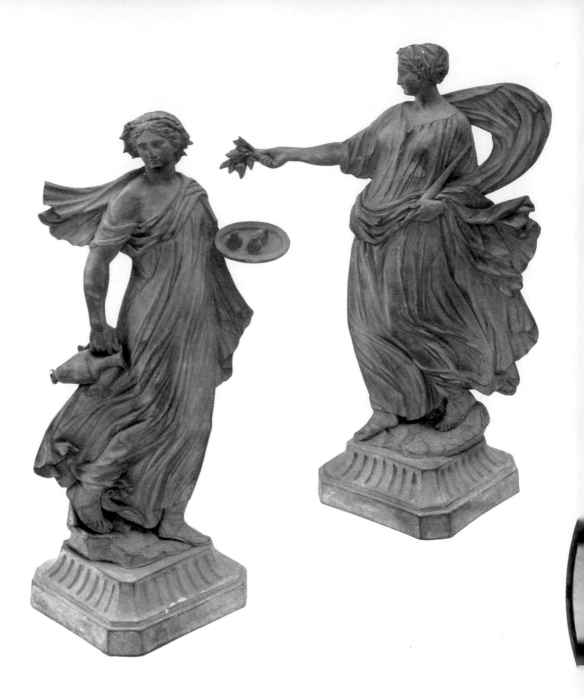

15. Pair of biscuit Queen's Ware statuettes named 'The Dancing Nymphs', c. 1770. The design was inspired by Pompeian frescos.

17. Queen's Ware cup and saucer, trial pieces for the service commissioned by the Empress Catherine of Russia in 1773. Saucer shows Stoke Gifford. *Mayer Collection, City of Liverpool Museums.*

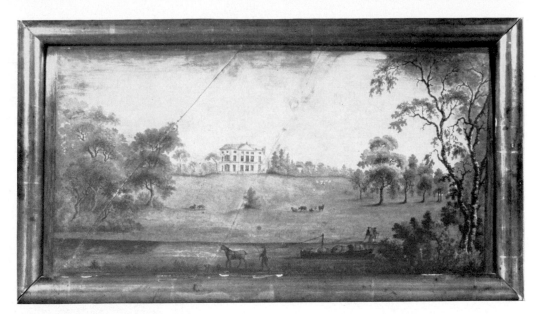

16. View of Etruria Hall, home of Josiah Wedgwood. Painted in enamels on a 'biscuit' (once-fired and unglazed) Queen's Ware plaque. Attributed to Edward Stringer, c. 1773.

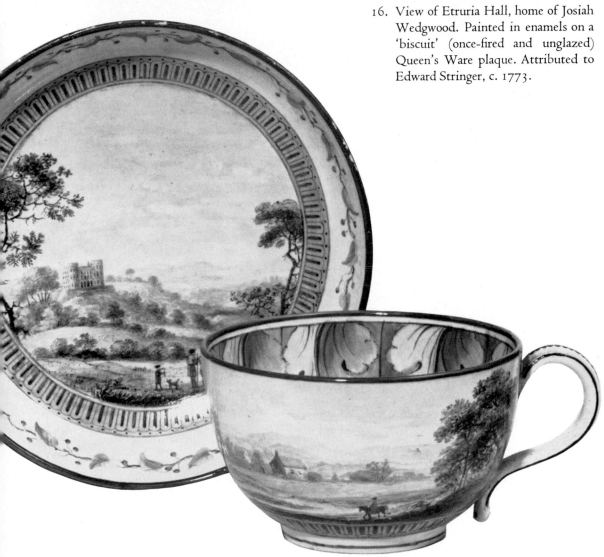

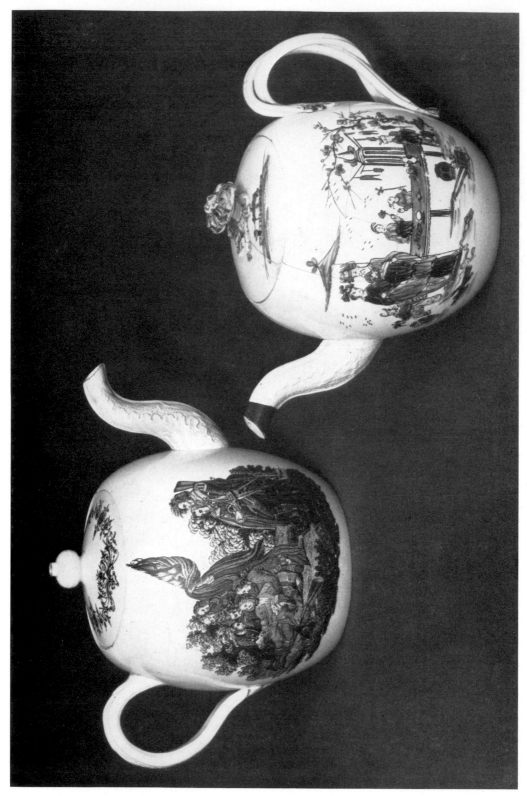

18. Queen's Ware teapots. Left, teapot with transfer printed scene depicting 'The Death of Wolfe', from painting by Benjamin West, c. 1780. Right, teapot decorated with 'chinoiseries', handpainted at Chelsea, c. 1770.

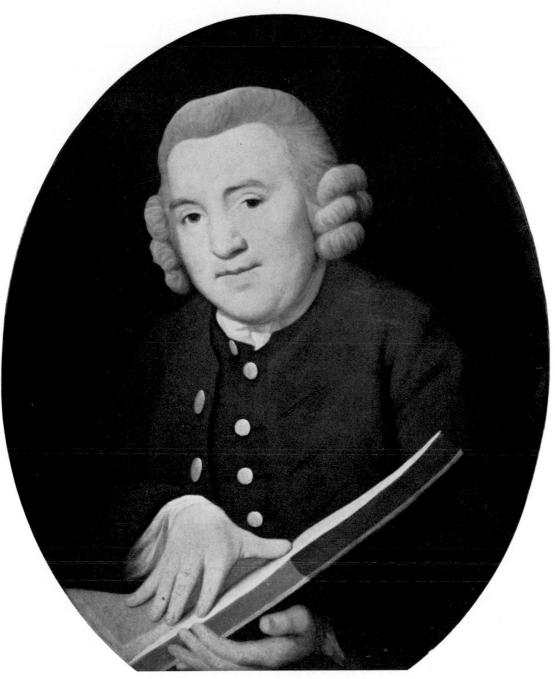

19. Portrait of the physician, Erasmus Darwin by
George Stubbs A.R.A. Painted in enamels
on an oval Queen's Ware plaque.
Size: 26 inches by 20
inches, dated 1783.

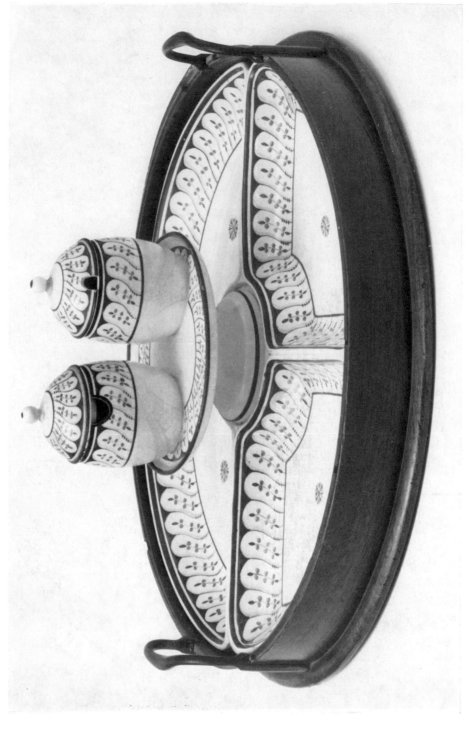

20. Queen's Ware sandwich set, fitted in contemporary tray, c. 1790. Decorated with brown and orange design illustrated in Wedgwood's first pattern book, begun in 1769.

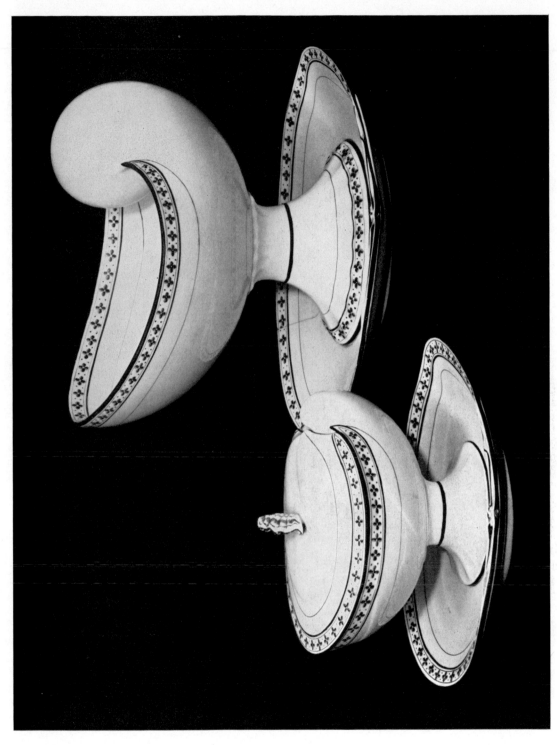

21. Two items from a Queen's Ware service in the 'Nautilus' shape, c. 1790. Decorated with Design No. 384 from Wedgwood's first pattern book.

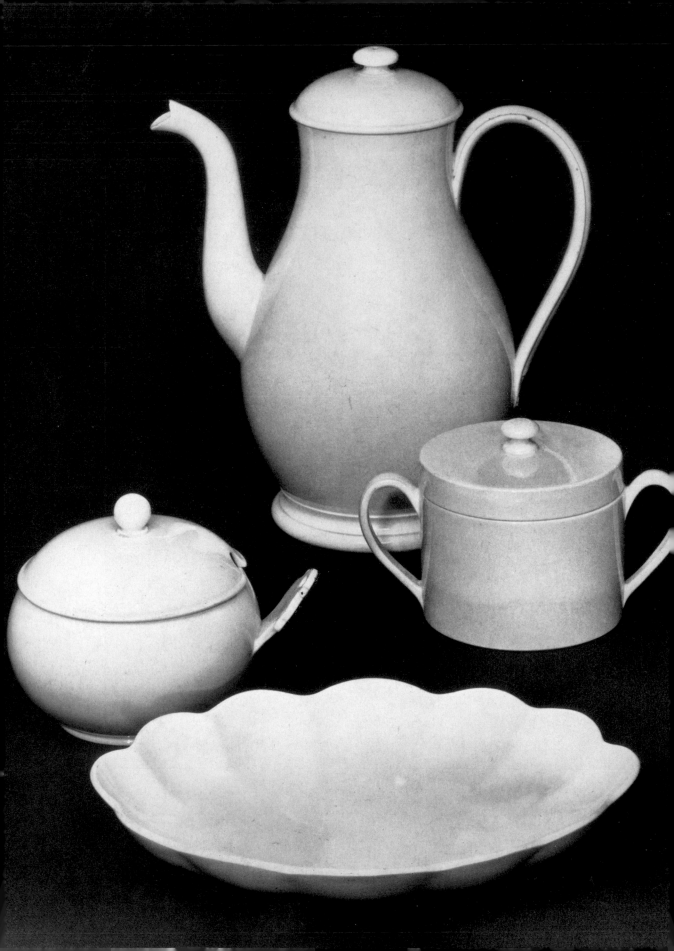

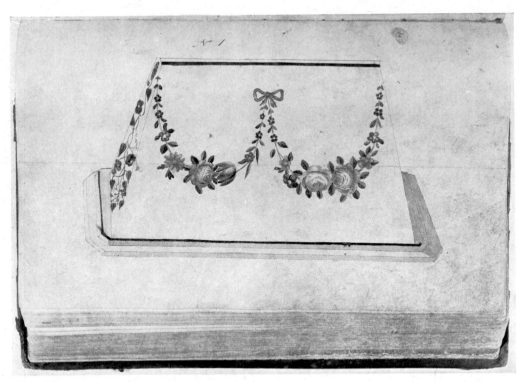

22. LEFT. Early period kitchen ware in Queen's Ware, c. 1790. Additional items in this undecorated cream-coloured range were introduced in the early part of the nineteenth century.

23. ABOVE. Drawing of a Queen's Ware jelly mould, illustrated in 1802 shape book. The jelly
moulds were in two parts: an undecorated container into which the liquid jelly was poured,
and a decorated cover of the same shape. When the jelly was set, the container was lifted
off before serving—and the jelly left to provide a purely decorative transparent casing to the
decorated wedge, cone or pyramid shape.

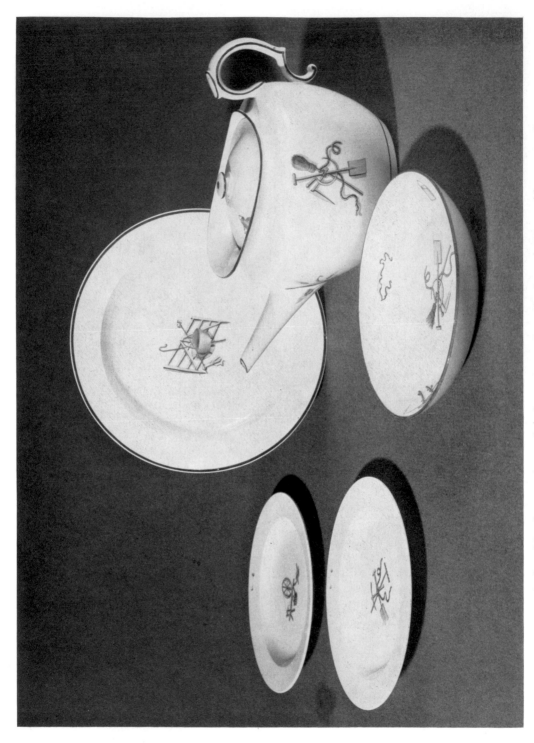

24. Agricultural implements are used as decoration on items in Queen's Ware tableware, c. 1805.

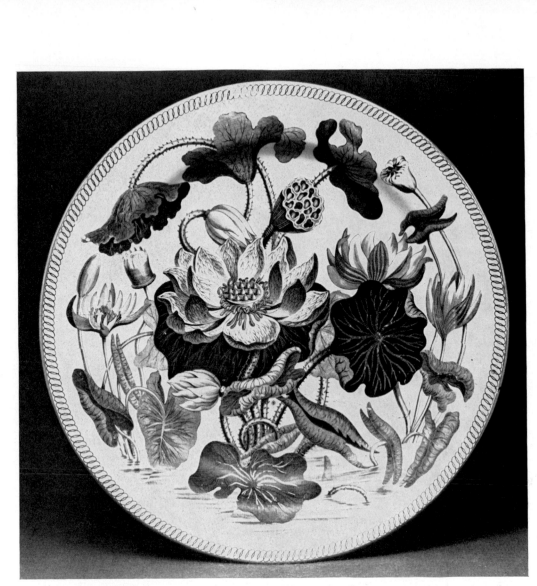

25. Queen's Ware plate decorated with 'Water Lily' pattern. This pattern originated in a service made by Josiah Wedgwood II for his sister, Susannah, in 1807. Susannah married Dr. Robert Waring Darwin, and they became the parents of Charles Darwin.

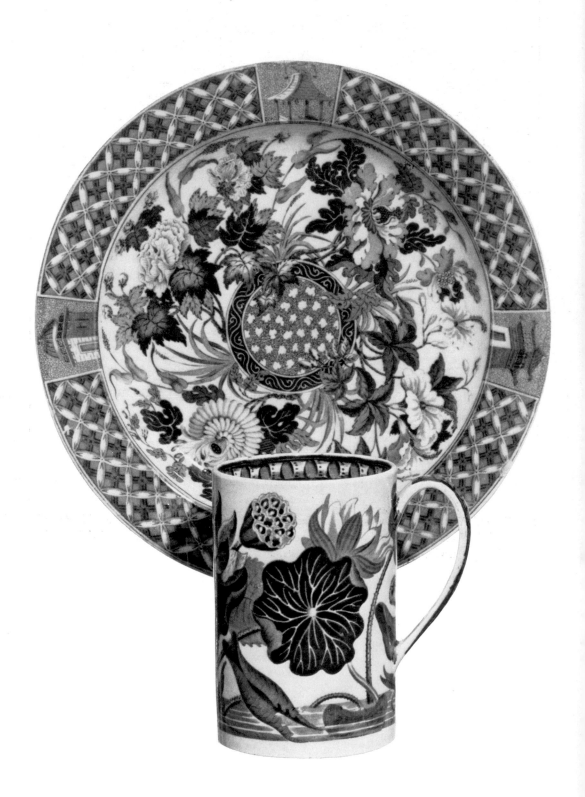

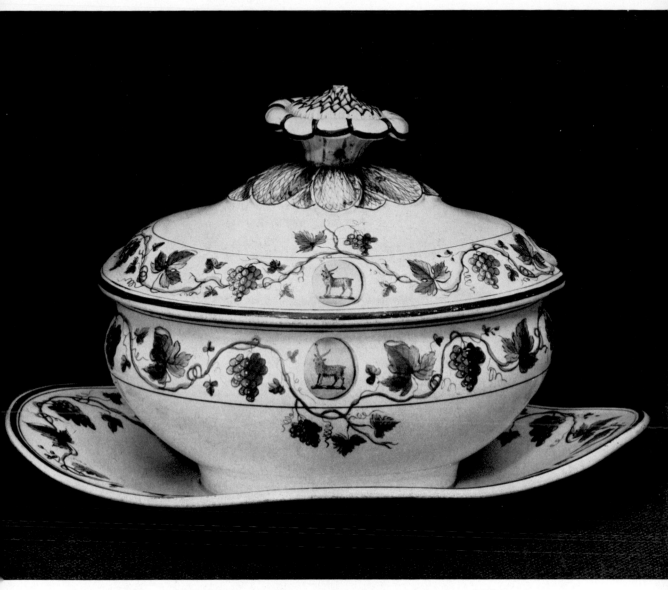

26. LEFT. Plate and jug in Queen's Ware, with underglaze decoration. 'Hibiscus' pattern decorates plate, and 'Water Lily' pattern is on jug. Both c. 1810.

27. ABOVE. Queen's Ware gravy dish and cover. From a service ordered by Lord William Russell in 1815. Decorated with 'Bedford Grape' pattern, and Lord William's crest in brown.

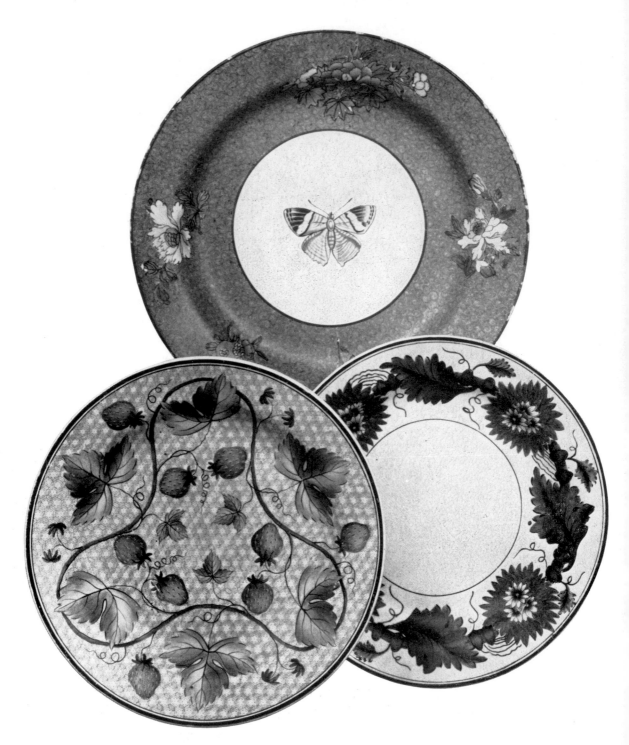

28. These plates illustrate three patterns used to decorate Queen's Ware services in the period 1820–30.

29. RIGHT. Potpourri container, bowl and jug in Queen's Ware, with drab (olive green) glaze. Lined and monogrammed in gold, c. 1820.

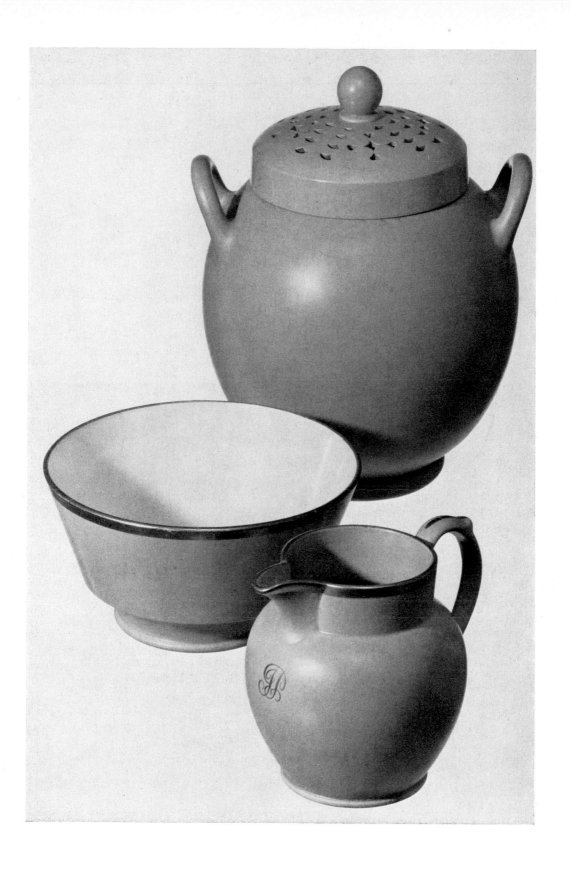

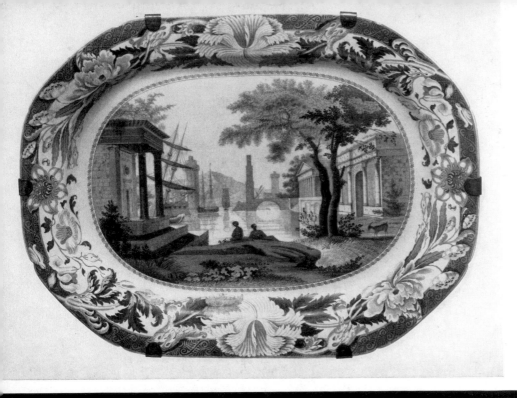

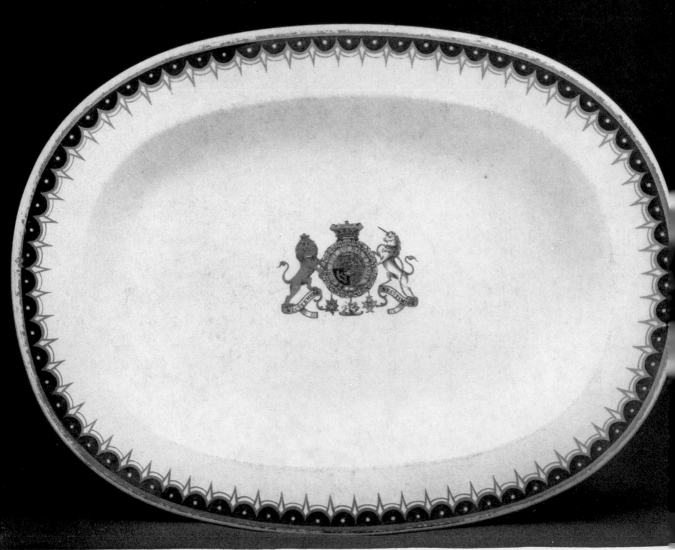

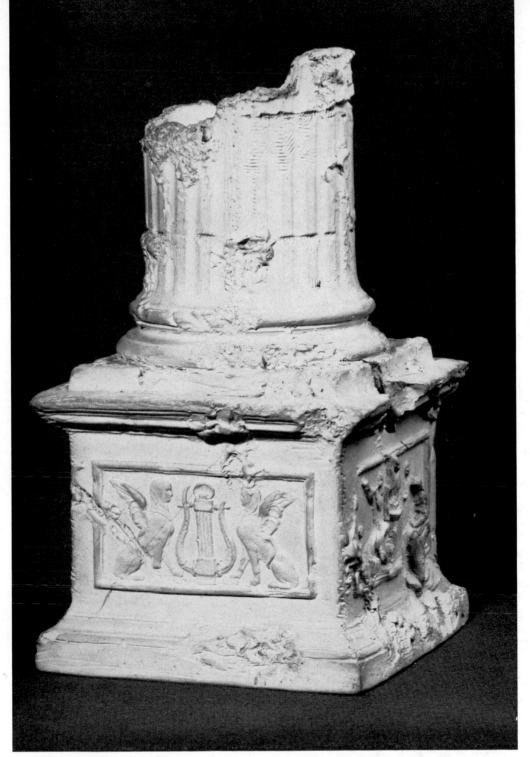

30. TOP LEFT. Stone china dish, decorated with underglaze 'Blue Claude' pattern, c. 1830.

31. LEFT. Dish from an armorial Queen's Ware service commissioned by the Duke of Clarence (later William IV) in 1821.

32. ABOVE. Ruined classical column in cane ware, decorated with reliefs of sphinxes, sacrifices, etc. around plinth, c. 1800. Reflects Georgian passion for dilapidated archaeological fragments.

33. BELOW. Cane ware cabaret service with hand-enamelled border pattern, c. 1790. The term 'cabaret' originally referred to a tea table, but came to mean a set of vessels comprising a small breakfast or tea service on a plateau (flat serving tray).

34. RIGHT. Inkwell in the form of a canopic jar. In cane ware, with applied brown reliefs in imitation of Egyptian hieroglyphics, c. 1800. *Manchester City Art Gallery.*

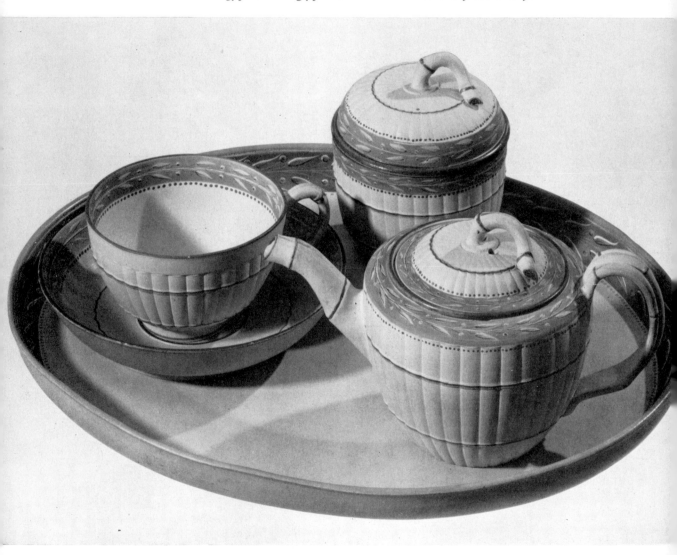

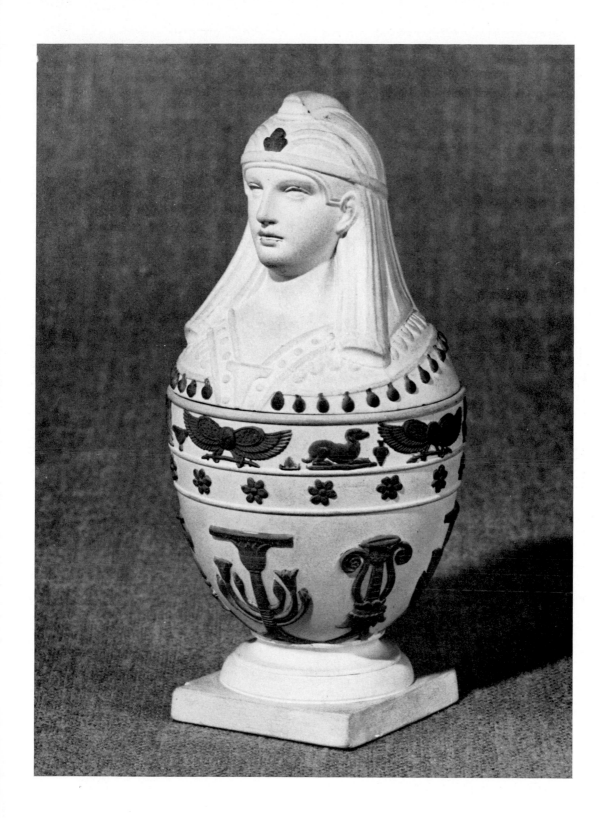

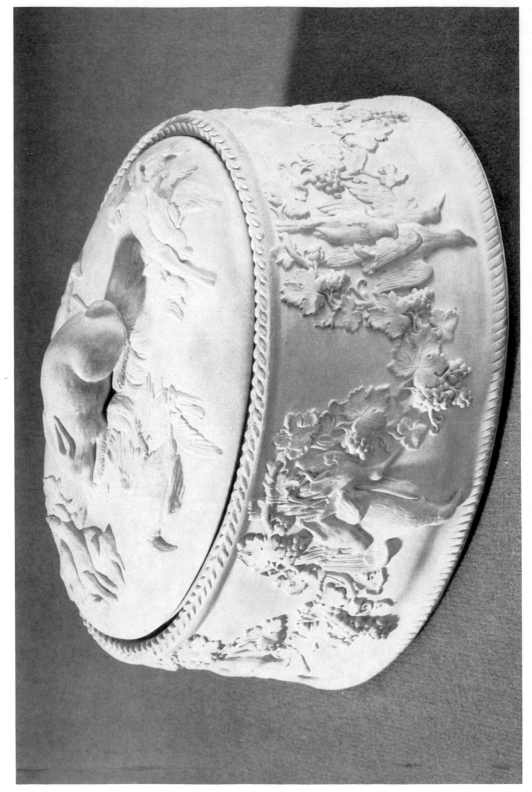

35. Game pie dish in cane ware, c. 1810. Unglazed, in a soft buff yellow—and made to resemble a pastry case. Game pie dishes were first produced in the early nineteenth century.

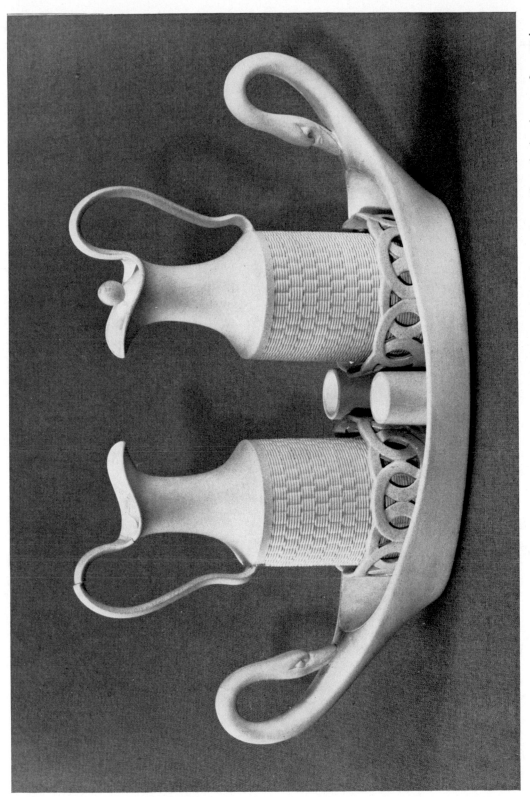

36. Cane ware oil and vinegar set, shaped to look like a boat with swan's head terminals. Basket work motif on the bottles, c. 1810. *Woburn Abbey Collection.*

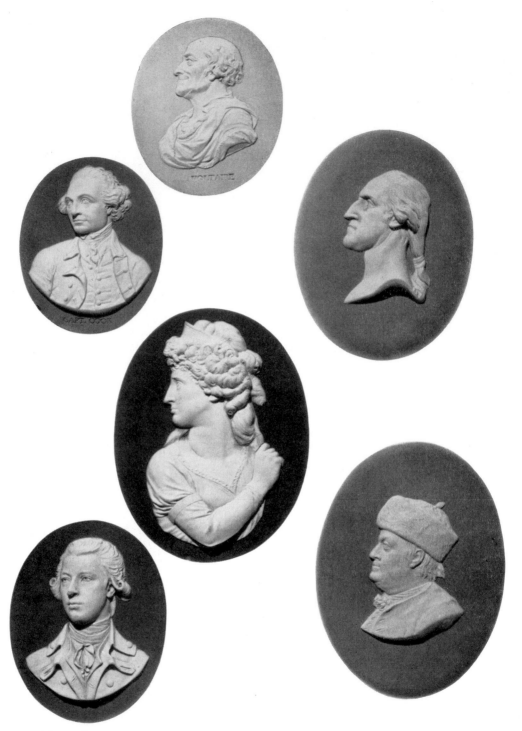

37. Eighteenth-century portrait medallions in Jasper. From top, and left to right, Voltaire, James Cook, George Washington, Sarah Siddons, William Pitt the Younger, Benjamin Franklin.

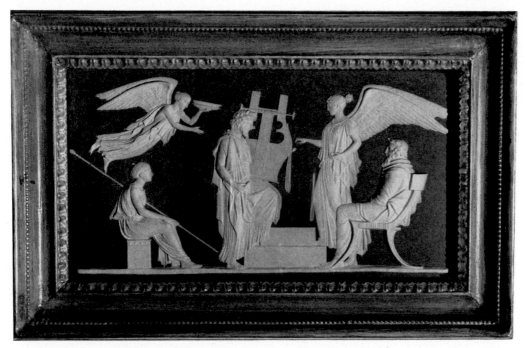

38. Jasper plaque, illustrating 'The Apotheosis of Homer', designed and modelled by John Flaxman RA. In white on dark blue, marked 'Wedgwood and Bentley'. Length 18 inches, c. 1778.

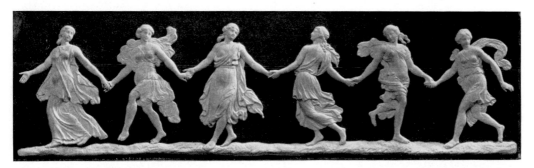

39. 'The Dancing Hours'—a Jasper frieze arranged in two panels, designed by John Flaxman and first mentioned by Wedgwood in April 1778. Originally meant for chimney piece use, this famous Wedgwood design has been applied to vases, bowls, etc. ever since.

40. A rook from Flaxman's Jasper chess set. The actor, John Philip Kemble, is said to have been the model for the kings, and the actress, Sarah Siddons, as Lady Macbeth, the model for the queens.

41. John Flaxman's original drawings for his chessmen, designed in 1784. Made in Jasper, the chessmen cost 5 guineas a set when first introduced.

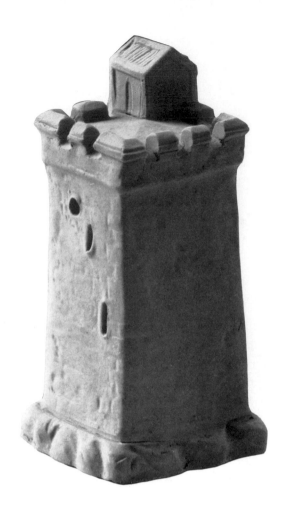

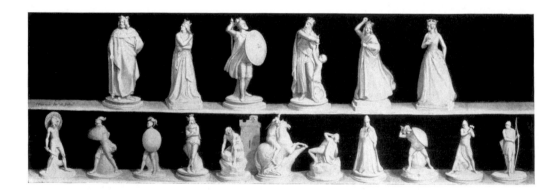

42. RIGHT. The 'Homer' vase, in white on dark blue Jasper. Modelled by John Flaxman in 1784 and depicting 'The Apotheosis of Homer'. Height: 18 inches.

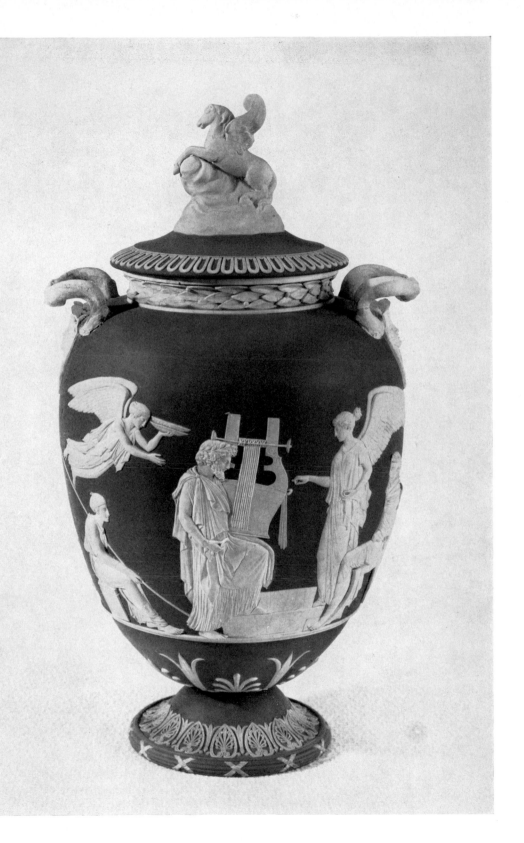

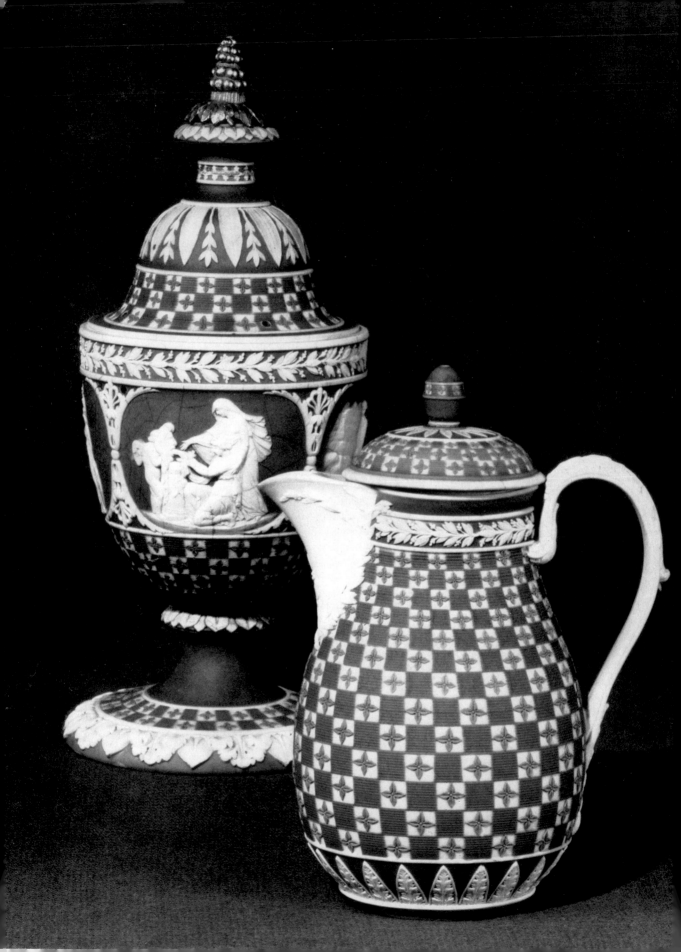

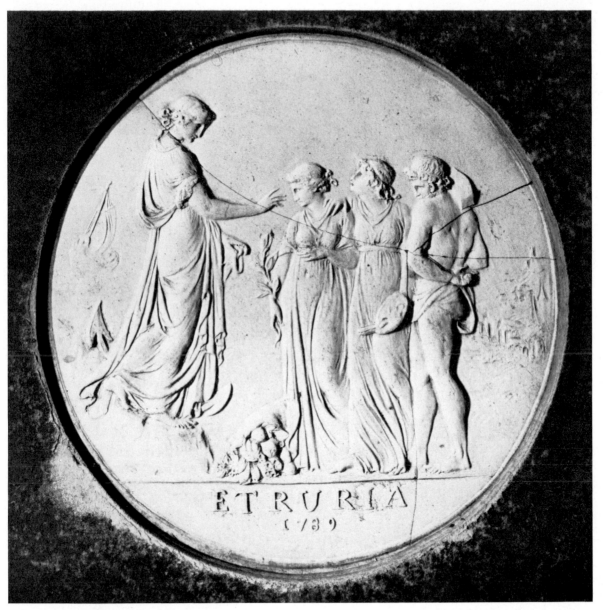

43. LEFT. Diced Jasper vase and jug. Both coloured in blue, green and white, c. 1785. *Manchester City Art Gallery.*

44. ABOVE. The Sydney Cove Medallion, in Jasper. Issued in 1789 to mark the foundation of Sydney. Contains Australian clay supplied by Arthur Phillip, first Governor of New South Wales, to the botanist Sir Joseph Banks.

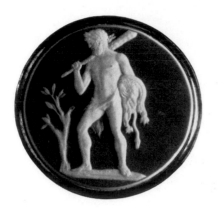

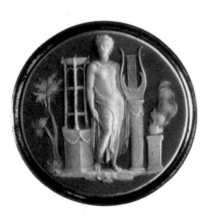

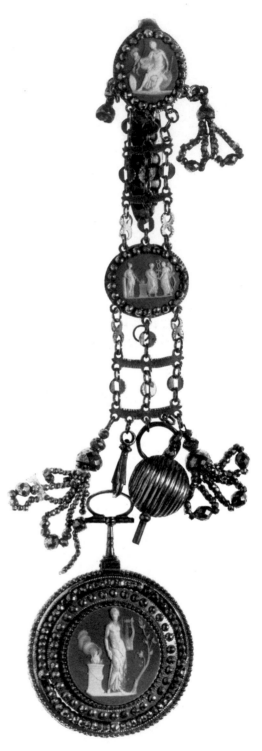

45. Two buttons, in white Jasper with blue dip (surface only colouring), c. 1790. The subjects are: top, Hercules, below, Apollo.

46. Chatelaine, or fob chain, with blue and white Jasper cameos mounted in cut steel, c. 1790.

47. FAR RIGHT. Two black and white Jasper vases from a garniture de cheminée, c. 1790. Decoration on vase, right, depicts 'The Chariot of Venus', while that on lefthand vase depicts 'Sacrifice to Ceres'.

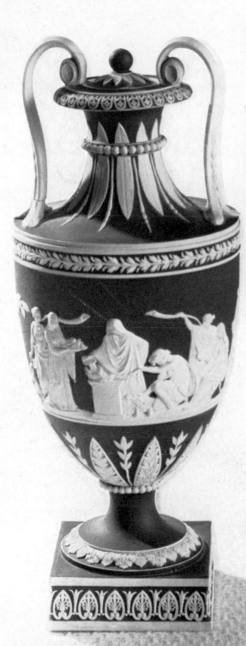
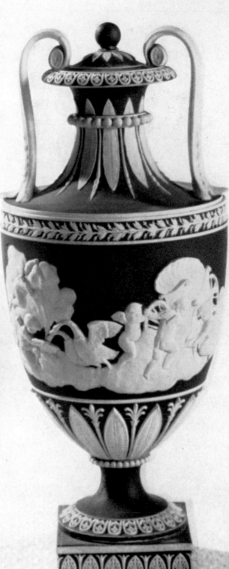

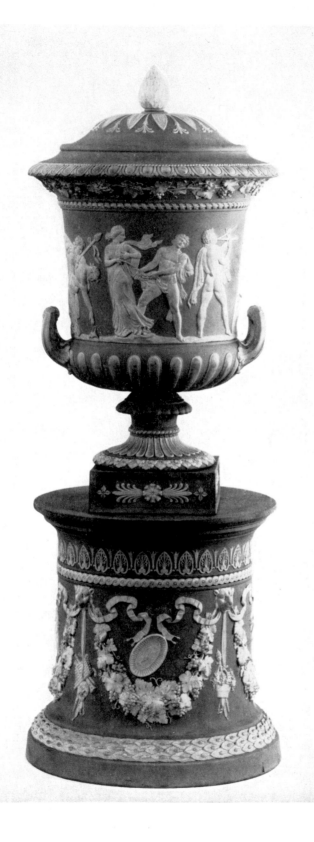

48. Blue Jasper vase on pedestal, c. 1850. Copy of famous Borghese Vase, with white relief decoration showing 'The Triumph of Bacchus'. *Wolverhampton City Art Gallery and Museum.*

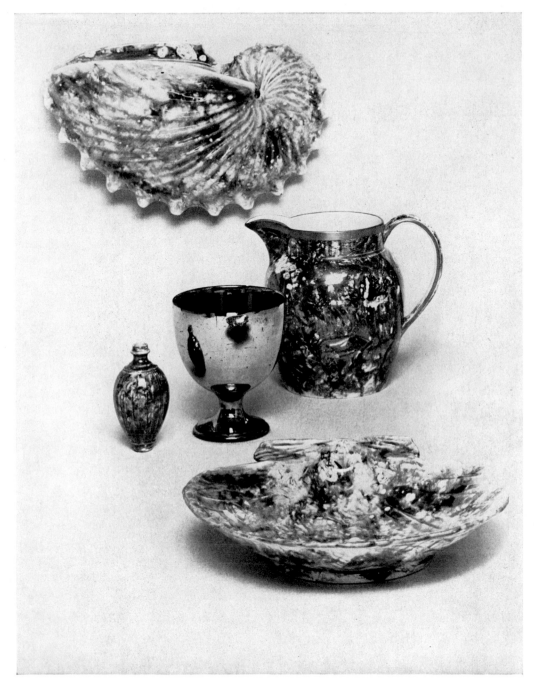

49. A selection of 'Moonlight' and 'Steel' lustre ware. 'Moonlight' was marbled pink, or purple and gold lustre, tinged with yellow and green; 'Steel' has a metallic appearance, both c. 1810.

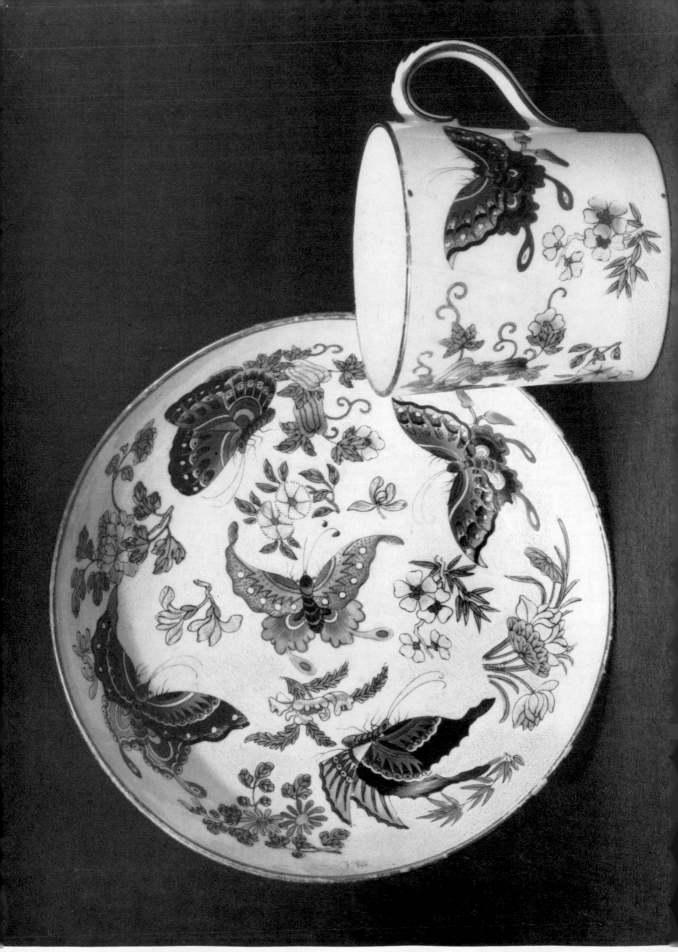

50. LEFT. First period bone china. Coffee can and saucer decorated in Wedgwood pattern No. 637: 'butterflies printed in black on glaze and flowers in brown, black, red and gold'. Marked 'Wedgwood' in red, c. 1815. *Mayer Collection, City of Liverpool Museums.*

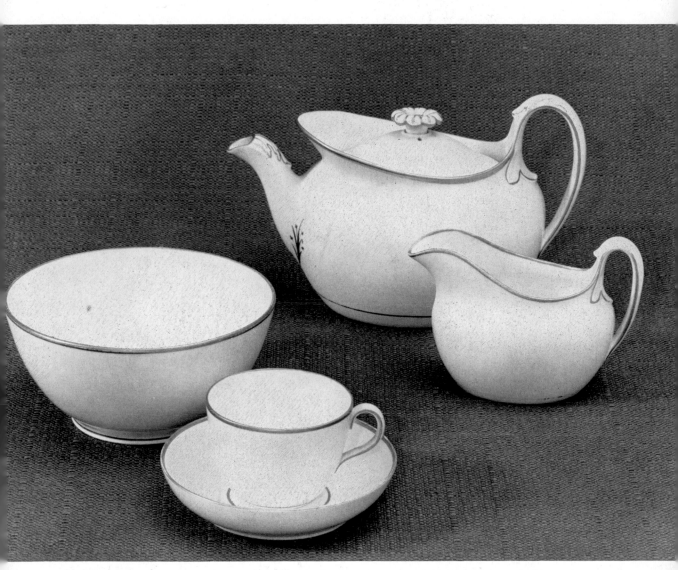

51. Fine bone china tea service items, including oval parapet teapot. Simply decorated in gold, c. 1815.

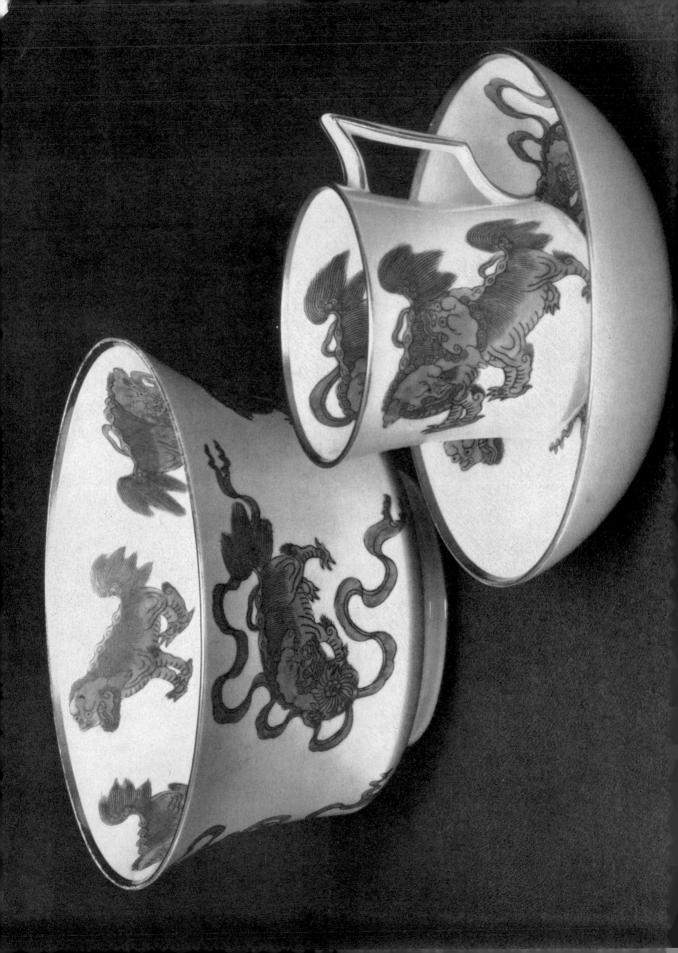

52. LEFT. 'Chinese Tigers', the name of a vivid green pattern, edged with gold. Used on fine bone china, c. 1815.

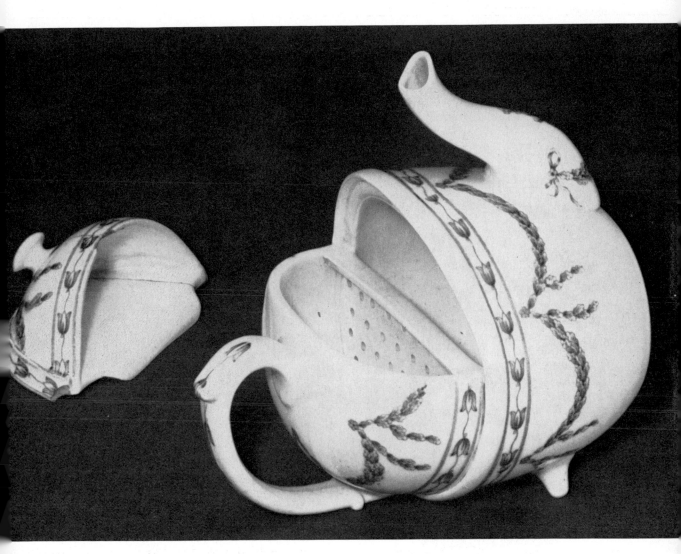

53. Simple Yet Perfect (SYP) teapot, c. 1907. An original teapot design introduced by Wedgwood in 1895. Hot water was poured through an opening near front of pot, falling below a horizontal perforated divider on which dry tea-leaves had been placed. When pot was tilted back, it rested on two legs and a curved handle, so that water passed through perforations into tea-leaves. After the tea had brewed, the pot was tilted forward onto the flat base, and liquid settled below the divider, ready to be poured out through the spout.

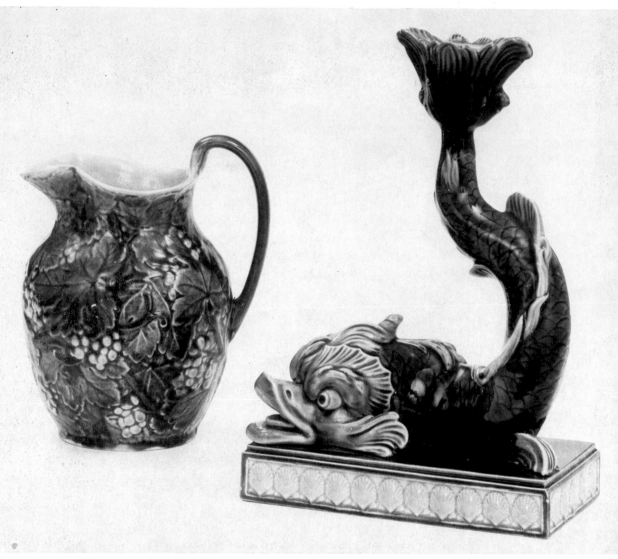

54. Queen's Ware jug and dolphin candlestick decorated with a so-called 'Majolica' glaze, c. 1865. Derived from a ware made in Majorca from the fifteenth century, this is a lead glaze stained with colouring oxides to give brilliant effects. It was introduced by Wedgwood in 1860.

55. Five items of Queen's Ware decorated by Emile Lessore, the eminent artist who worked for Wedgwood in England, 1858–63—and continued to decorate Queen's Ware after his return to France.

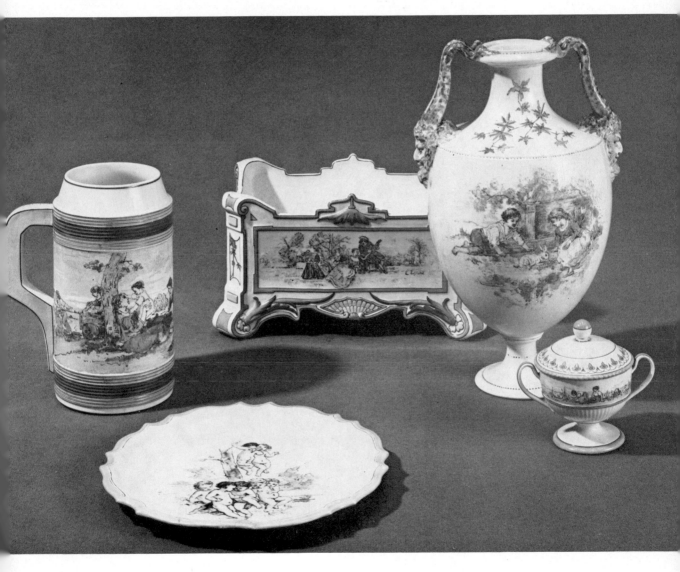

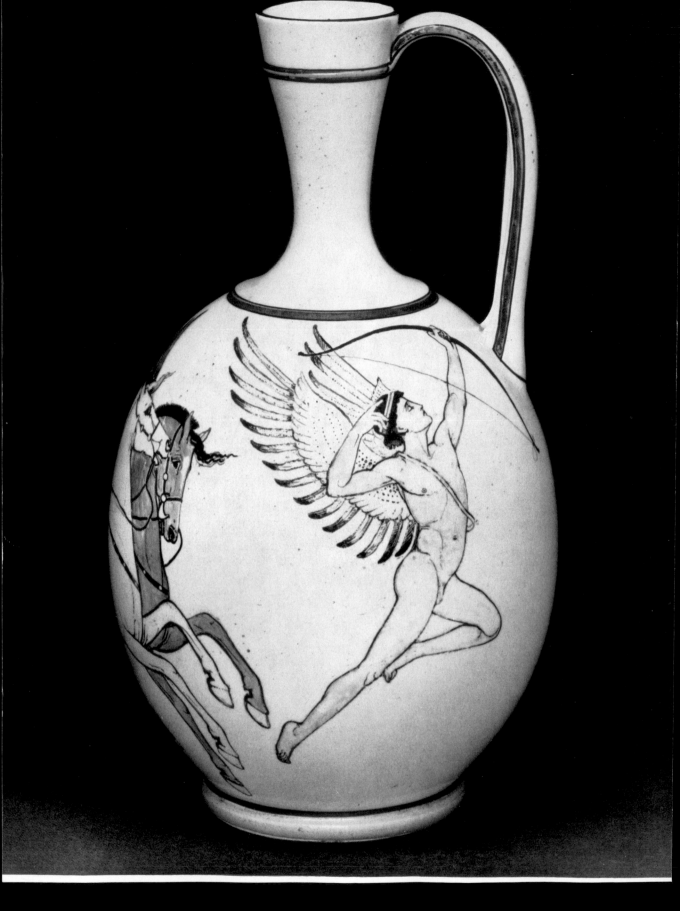

56. 'Ambition' is the title of this hand-enamelled design, on a Queen's Ware vase, by the painter, Walter Crane. Executed in 1870.

57. Bowl and vases in 'Fairyland Lustre' and 'Dragon Ware'. This lustre ware was made in the period 1914–39, with decoration by Daisy Makeig-Jones. 'Fairyland Lustre' designs depict whimsical creatures in fairyland settings. Colours are markedly iridescent and no pieces are identical.

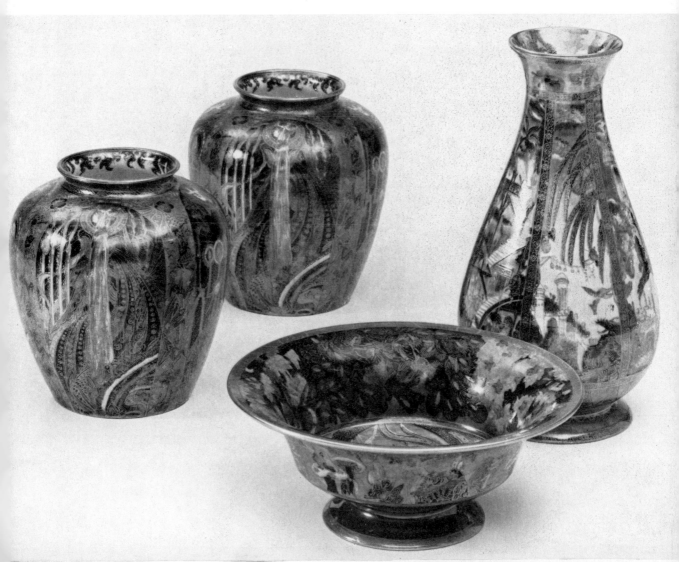

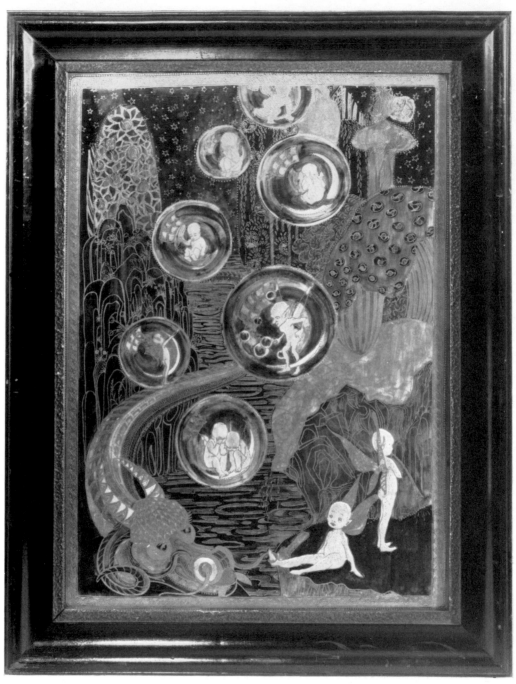

58. 'Fairyland Lustre' plaque entitled 'Bubbles'. Designed by Daisy Makeig-Jones c. 1920.

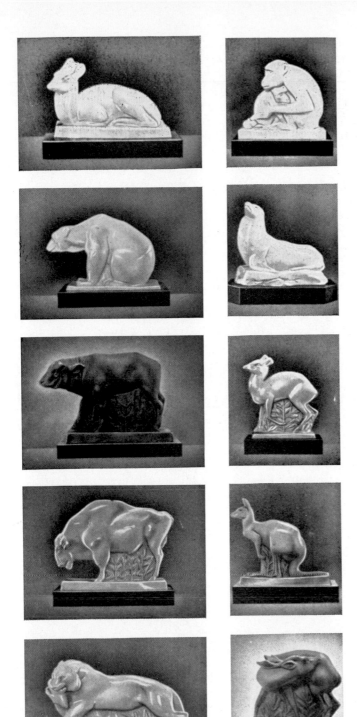

59. Queen's Ware animals, modelled by the sculptor John Skeaping. Produced in the 1930s. Picture from a contemporary catalogue of the period.

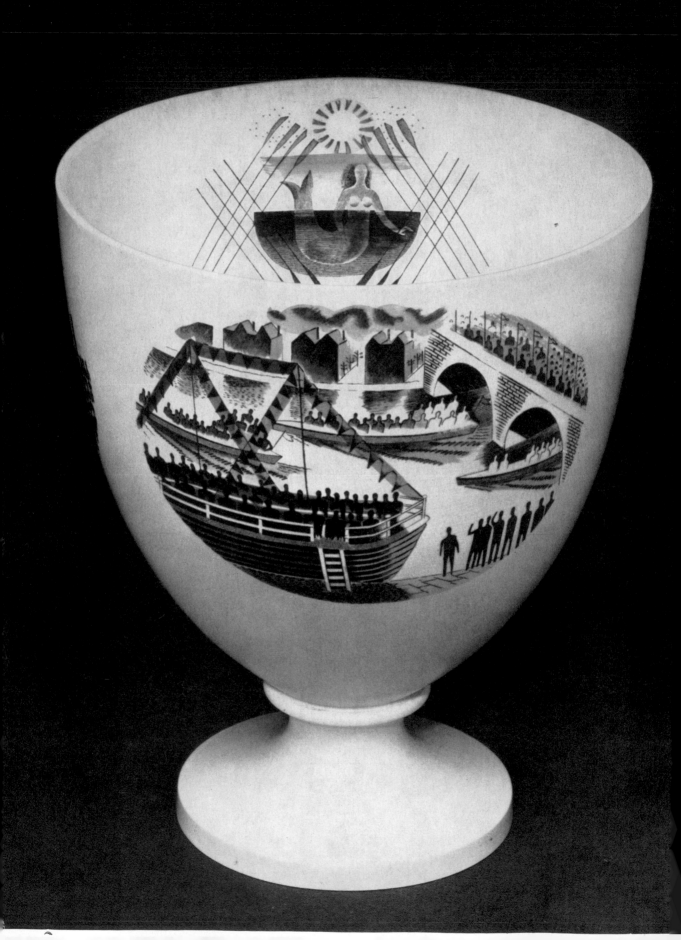

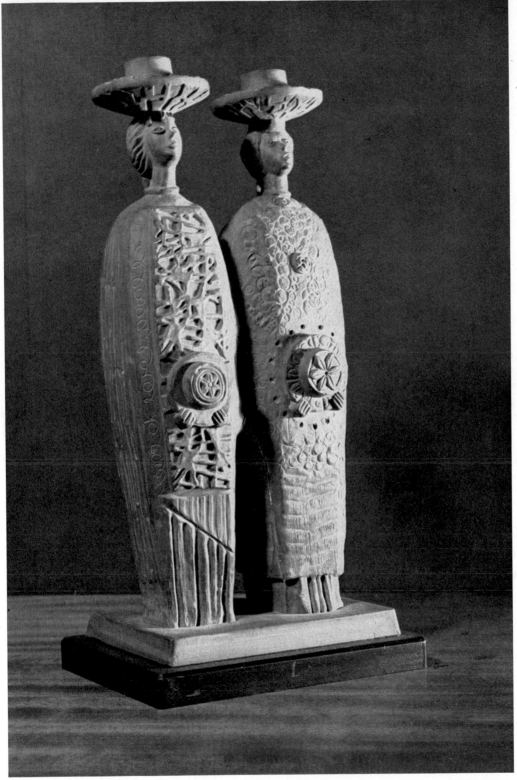

60. LEFT. The Boat Race cup, decorated with multi-coloured printed design on Queen's Ware.
Designed by Eric Ravilious, with bowl bearing same design, in 1938.

61. ABOVE. 'The Mexicans'—a pair of candlesticks designed by Professor Angelo Biancini.
Produced in terracotta and Black Basalt, in 1962.

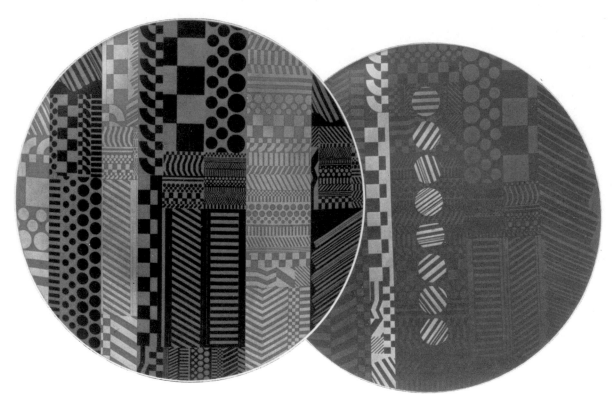

62. Two designs from 'Variations on a Geometric Theme', a set of six plates designed by the sculptor and graphic artist, Eduardo Paolozzi. Intricately coloured on fine bone china. Issued in limited, numbered edition of 200 sets in 1970.